T0318627

"Mark DeLuzio merges the basics of running an excellent business with the basics of developing an excellent lean enterprise. If you are *truly* interested in success, it lies in *Flatlined*."

Jim Huntzinger, President and Founder, Lean Frontiers

"In addition to offering executives a concise, step-wise plan for reviving comatose Lean efforts, *Flatlined* will also be useful to leaders who are new to Lean management."

Dr. Bob Emiliani, Professor of Lean Leadership, Author

"As Lean Management rapidly approaches its tipping point, Mark DeLuzio is the right person to give it a final nudge. Whether you want to jump to the front of the leadership line or leapfrog your company's transition to greatness, read *Flatlined* now. You will never think about organizational life in the same way again."

Jim Hudson, author of *The 21 Invincible Laws of Lean Leadership*

"Through Mark DeLuzio's unique experience in the Lean community, he has learned what does and doesn't work in any business environment."

Jerry Solomon, Former Vice President, MarquipWardUnited;
Lean Accounting Pioneer

"Mark DeLuzio stands among the pioneers in his field as living proof of the power of Continuous Improvement—even after 30 years as a practitioner and advisor."

Clifford F. Ransom II, President of Ransom Research, Inc.

FLATLINED
Why Lean Transformations Fail and What to Do About It

Mark C. DeLuzio

Routledge
Taylor & Francis Group

A PRODUCTIVITY PRESS BOOK

First published 2020
by Routledge
52 Vanderbilt Avenue, New York, NY 10017

and by Routledge
2 Park Square, Milton Park, Abingdon, Oxon, OX14 4RN

Routledge is an imprint of the Taylor & Francis Group, an informa business

© 2020 Mark C. DeLuzio

The right of Mark C. DeLuzio to be identified as author of this work has been asserted by him in accordance with sections 77 and 78 of the Copyright, Designs and Patents Act 1988.

All rights reserved. No part of this book may be reprinted or reproduced or utilized in any form or by any electronic, mechanical, or other means, now known or hereafter invented, including photocopying and recording, or in any information storage or retrieval system, without permission in writing from the publishers.

Trademark notice: Product or corporate names may be trademarks or registered trademarks, and are used only for identification and explanation without intent to infringe.

Library of Congress Cataloging-in-Publication Data
Names: DeLuzio, Mark C., author.
Title: Flatlined : why lean transformations fail and what to do about it / Mark C. DeLuzio.
Description: New York, NY : Routledge, 2020. | Includes bibliographical references and index.
Identifiers: LCCN 2019052627 (print) | LCCN 2019052628 (ebook) | ISBN 9780367247782 (paperback) | ISBN 9780367247799 (hardback) | ISBN 9780429284342 (ebook)
Subjects: LCSH: Organizational effectiveness. | Organizational change. | Cost control–Management. | Quality control–Management.
Classification: LCC HD58.9 .D454 2020 (print) | LCC HD58.9 (ebook) | DDC 658.4/013–dc23
LC record available at https://lccn.loc.gov/2019052627
LC ebook record available at https://lccn.loc.gov/2019052628

ISBN: 978-0-367-24779-9 (hbk)
ISBN: 978-0-367-24778-2 (pbk)
ISBN: 978-0-429-28434-2 (ebk)

Typeset in Minion
by Wearset Ltd, Boldon, Tyne and Wear

Your company is already perfectly engineered to realize the results you've recently achieved.

–Mark C. DeLuzio

Contents

Foreword

Ever since Western companies began adopting the Toyota Production System (TPS, or Lean) in the early 1980s, two key questions have always stood out:

1. Why are so many CEOs/companies reluctant to start down the Lean path?
2. Even when they do initiate a Lean transformation and enjoy early success, why do most companies' Lean efforts eventually flatline and, in many cases, eventually go backwards?

In fact, although there are no definitive statistics, it is generally believed that only 5–7% of the companies that start down the Lean path ever get to the state where they could be called a Lean enterprise. For a management approach that is as close to magic as any you will ever find, this is a shocking failure rate.

There are all kinds of reasons/theories as to why CEOs are reluctant to even begin with Lean, and my guess is that we can debate this forever without establishing a rationale with which most people will agree. It's more productive and timely to address the issue of why so many companies that do start Lean, and have some early success, eventually flatline. Defining the problem here and providing the proper solutions to get back on track will help more companies. That is why this book is so important and such a great contribution to the Lean movement worldwide.

The author, Mark C. DeLuzio, is one of the best Lean minds anywhere and has decades of experience to back it up. His straightforward reasons for why Lean companies flatline in their Lean implementations are right on the money:

1. They see Lean as just a short-term tactical tool.
2. The company's Lean efforts are not connected to its overall strategy.
3. They optimize functions but not the enterprise.
4. Leadership is either hands-off or unwilling to revisit its basics.

If any of these reasons seem familiar to what is happening in your own company, this book is a must-read for you. In my experience, and I have been implementing Lean in various companies since early 1982, a very high percentage of companies (could be over 90%) see Lean mainly as a cost reduction tool and start down the Lean path with this as the primary goal. This is Mark's point number one above. They will get results, because it is almost impossible not to, but will generally never get out of what we could call the "tools" stage of Lean and will flatline fairly quickly. They will treat Lean as "some manufacturing or operations thing" and will never engage the rest of the organization. In fact, they will put the various parts of the organization in even greater conflict than before they started Lean.

But the beauty of this book is Mark's detailed, step-by-step explanation of what to do to overcome a flatlined state and get back on track. The first step is shifting the mindset away from, "But we're different, Lean doesn't apply to us." I think it was Henry Ford who said, "Whether you think you can, or you think you can't, you'll be right." So, as Mark covers, getting leaders to see Lean as a strategic growth strategy and not just cost reduction is an important shift. He uses some great examples/case studies to illustrate his points. In this case, he uses a Danaher acquisition that had a 28-day lead time versus 35 days for the competition. As a result, they felt they had clear industry leadership and didn't need this Lean stuff. Of course, they were now a part of Danaher so that wasn't an option. In roughly 18 months, they took lead time down to 3 days from 28, on-time delivery from 30% to over 96%, and inventory turns from 2x to 18x. The net result was they tripled the size of the business.

Mark also shares how to align Lean with the company's strategy and why this is important. He shows the way to make Lean an enterprise endeavor as opposed to the more common point kaizen approach to solving problems. He has a great section on traditional accounting, for example, explaining why this can be such a drag on results and why it needs to be changed. At the end of each chapter, Mark provides a very clear checklist of questions to ask yourself. So, if your company has flatlined its Lean initiative, here lies the recipe to get back on track—and you will no longer have the excuse that you didn't know what to do.

But why listen to Mark C. DeLuzio? Back when I was a Group Executive at The Danaher Corporation, one of the companies for which I was responsible was Jacobs Engine Brake (commonly known as Jake Brake). The President of Jake Brake was a guy named George Koenigsaecker. My office was in the Jake Brake building, and George and I were the only two people in Danaher at the time with some prior TPS (Lean) experience. Jake Brake was in bad shape and we decided to use a Lean strategy to turn it around. Early on, we hired Mark C. DeLuzio to be Jake's CFO and off we went. We utilized the Shingijutsu Consulting Company from Japan. They were all ex-Toyota guys who taught us the Toyota approach. We were their only US client for the first four years. Mark quickly got involved in our Lean efforts and learned directly from the Shingijutsu consultants. A few years later, after George and I had both left Danaher, Mark became head of the Lean efforts across all of Danaher and is really the father of the now famous Danaher Business System (DBS). He had years of experience integrating a series of acquisitions smoothly into Danaher and the DBS approach. Oh, and by the way, Jake Brake over the first ten years of Lean grew sales from $65 million to $220 million without adding any physical space and only 25 extra people. The number of brakes per man hour grew from 3 to 35, inventory turns went from 2x to 25x, lead time dropped from 85 days to 2 days, and operating income went from 4% to more than 35%. For the past 18 years, Mark has led Lean Horizons Consulting, gaining extensive experience implementing Lean across a wide array of companies.

I went on to become the CEO of The Wiremold Company, where over the course of 9+ years we more than quadrupled sales, cut lead times from 6 weeks to 2 days, increased inventory turns from 2x to 18x, increased operating income by 13.4x and enterprise value by just under 2,500%. I have since been an operating partner in a private equity firm where we used Lean across the portfolio to improve results and have authored two books, *The Lean Turnaround* (McGraw-Hill Education, 2012) and *The Lean Turnaround Action Guide* (McGraw-Hill Education, 2016). I am a member of the *Industry Week Magazine* Manufacturing Hall of Fame, the AME (American Manufacturing Excellence) hall of fame and the Shingo Academy (the Shingo Prize's version of a hall of fame).

I have known Mark for a long time and can't think of anyone better qualified to get you out of a flatlined state if that's where you find yourself. Just follow the template he has laid out for you in this book, and you will soon have results that equal, if not exceed, Jake Brake and Wiremold.

– Art Byrne

Author of *The Lean Turnaround* and *The Lean Tunraround Action Guide*,

former Danaher Corporation executive,

former Wiremold CEO,

the Pacific Ocean on a cruise from Kobe, Japan to Vancouver, June 2019

Preface

Why would I add to all that's been written about Lean? There are plenty of good books that teach the tools of Lean. Instead, this book makes the case for the need to connect Lean to the business as a whole—to tie it to strategy, use it enterprise-wide, and embed it into the culture. This is important because when this doesn't happen, businesses will flatline with their Lean efforts over time.

Although this book will be helpful for new users of Lean to put what they are learning into the context of a larger business strategy, it's aimed at those who have been in the trenches with Lean for a long time. Instead of providing a cookie-cutter approach to establishing a Lean program from scratch in a newly formed organization, this book will help you make needed changes to what already exists because it isn't working anymore. Your company is already engineered to get the results you are getting. Odds are that you picked up this book because you are not happy with those results and are wanting a better framework to reevaluate everything you are doing.

In a brownfield environment, it's much more difficult to change the way Lean is thought about. It's akin to fixing a train while it's moving down the track at 80 miles an hour. The system redesign has to happen in a constantly moving, chaotic state.

This book also serves as a reminder that Lean can be a comprehensive solution to your business problems if you honor the integrity of it. The failure rate is only high on Lean for those who aren't really adhering to Lean principles, and there is a lot of confusion today. When I started learning Lean in 1988, there weren't thousands of consultants and "experts" out there trying to make a name for themselves by promoting the next thing. Now there's Toyoda Kata in a Box. We weren't in the thick of the Information Age. Now, type Lean management, manufacturing, or process into a search engine and the results are overwhelming. How do you know what's a good source of information when the messaging has become so diluted?

I'm Mark C. DeLuzio, and I'm the principle architect of the Danaher Business System (DBS) and considered the father of Lean accounting. In the 1990s, we created DBS at Danaher in an effort to create a world-class industrial organization. DBS is now considered to be the flagship model of Lean in the United States. Toyota gets a lot of well-deserved coverage in the Lean space and we were certainly benchmarking them, often traveling to Japan to learn from the originators of the Toyota Production System.

I thought you should finally have the insider knowledge of what we learned and developed at Danaher so you can better benchmark Danaher. I also want you to get this correct information directly from the source—from someone who learned straight from the masters. Sometimes Lean knowledge gets passed down and, like the children's game of telephone, the message at the end gets translated differently or watered down. My hope is that these insights will not only help you turn around your Lean efforts, but will prevent you from making some of the mistakes that we did as we were figuring it out.

The spark of what we developed for Jake Brake (a division of Danaher) became embedded into the entire culture at Danaher, cementing the foundation that enabled it to become one of the top-performing companies in the world and never flatline. It also gave rise to the modern Lean movement that was adopted by hundreds of companies, such as United Technologies and GE.

After 13 years at Danaher, I left to launch my consulting practice, Lean Horizons Consulting. For the past 18 years, my team and I have worked with all types of businesses—from oil and gas fracking to insurance to financial services to pharmaceutical to automotive to aerospace to diversified industrials—to help them get better results from their Lean initiatives. Most, if not all, of these companies were making the same mistakes over and over again. After being involved in literally hundreds of Lean transformation initiatives, I started noticing a pattern. Many companies had initial success, then they "flatlined" and failed to continue or sustain the results they had achieved.

Around 2010, I started getting phone calls from CEOs who had been practicing Lean in their companies for over a decade. They were saying, "Mark, we're no longer getting the kinds of results we've previously seen using Lean, and we've tried to figure out why this is happening, but we have no idea." Or, "We had a lot of early wins with Lean and we are left wondering where they went."

They were also saying their problems were unique to their business, but I was seeing the same types of concerns arising in companies across the broad landscape of industries we serve. After a number of these types of calls and our efforts to turn this around for them, I wanted to document what we've found as to the consistent reasons why these companies are flatlining after a decade or more, and what to do about it.

In the first two chapters, I share the four primary reasons that companies are now flatlining with Lean and give you the outline for my five-step solution. The balance of this book gets into each of those steps in more depth, giving you a way to rethink your Lean process and culture and take actions that will get your company going in the right direction again—all while daily operations have to keep moving forward. At the end of each chapter, you'll find the questions you should be asking yourself and your team.

It is my wish that by reading this book and implementing what you learn, you will accelerate your organization's journey toward world-class status.

Acknowledgments

I have been influenced by many Japanese teachers, but I must recognize my mentors, Mr. Yoshiki Iwata and Chihiro Nakao of Shingijutsu, who have inspired me to dedicate my career to Lean. Their mentorship and teachings have had an everlasting impression on me. They have fired me often, only to welcome me back! They have labeled me a "cement head" many times, but through their coaching, they were able to soften this head, preparing me for a life of converting other cement heads. In the early days, Nakao-San told me that I am a disciple of Taiichi Ohno and I must dedicate my life to Lean. In 2016, when I saw him last, he remembered the conversation and thanked me for carrying on with Ohno's legacy. I cannot overstate the impact that these two men have had on my personal and professional life. But I will leave you with one lesson that Nakao-San taught me. He said: "DeLuzio-San, do not do kaizen at home. Wife gets very mad!"

I would also like to thank Steve and Mitch Rales, the founders of Danaher, along with Danaher's first CEO, George Sherman, for giving me the opportunity to become the architect of the famed Danaher Business System.

I would be remiss if I did not mention Art Byrne. Art was responsible for bringing Lean to Danaher and the United States in general. Little did we know that we would be creating history. Art took these concepts to Wiremold, which has been recognized as one of the most successful Lean transformations in history. Art is a true pioneer of the Lean movement, and I thank him for his mentorship and friendship.

I also need to thank George Koenigsaecker, who, as President of Jake Brake, hired me into his financial organization and eventually promoted me to CFO. George gave me the opportunity to study Lean in Japan with the renowned consulting group Shingijutsu. When I returned from Japan, I was convinced that my future was no longer in finance. I needed to be a part of what would become the Lean movement. Thirty years later, I haven't left the field. George is a visionary and my learning never stopped when I worked for George.

Bob Pentland is the unsung hero of Jake Brake's remarkable transformation. Bob was the Vice President of Operations working for George, and was the one who brought George's vision to life. As I developed the first Lean accounting system in the United States, both Bob and George were extremely supportive and encouraged me in my endeavor. Bob was one of the best Lean teachers I've had, and the lessons he taught me are part of my Lean DNA.

Writing a book is not an easy endeavor. It is a time commitment that takes away from family and personal time. So, I would like to thank my wife Diane, for her love and support during this project. In our 39 years of marriage, she has always been supportive of my career despite the fact it took me away to 45 countries over the years.

Lastly, I would like to thank Kirsten Vernon (BrandedBio.com), who was an invaluable asset to me in the writing of this book. She understood my goals and executive brand, positioned my vision in a book proposal, asked challenging questions, and provided me with a process to organize my thoughts. This book would not be what it is without her skills.

About the Author

Mark C. DeLuzio—known as a pioneer of Lean and the principal architect of the Danaher Business System (DBS)—serves as a trusted advisor to senior leaders in global organizations whose financial and operation metrics have flatlined. Leveraging his unmatched and inventive experience, Mark helps them think differently about how to optimize their approach system-wide. For his winning record in transforming companies and facilitating non-zero-sum game deals, Mark also served on the board of Hillenbrand Inc. (NYSE: HI) for 11 years.

HANDS-ON IMPLEMENTATION THAT DRIVES SUSTAINABLE RESULTS

While many know Lean in theory, Mark has lived it inside and out in practice. After developing the first Lean accounting process in the US for Danaher's Jake Brake division—setting an industry standard many companies are still trying to replicate—Mark became the VP of Danaher Business Systems, where he led its global deployment and enlightened Wall Street on its merits. Engaged in their first study mission to Japan to learn from Toyota and its suppliers, he's still mentored by the masters of the Toyota Production System today. Fundamental in Danaher's recognition as one of the leading implementers of Lean, Mark founded Lean Horizons Consulting in 2001 to helm a global team that serves clients on five continents in both specific and broad business applications of Lean. Their hallmark project with GE's Money Division—which generated $216 million in its first year by reducing retail credit card processing approvals to one day from 63—was profiled in *Harvard Business Review*. In 2007, Mark's "Excellence in Manufacturing" contributions were recognized when he was inducted as a Life Member of the Shingo Prize Academy, the "Hall of Fame" for Lean leaders.

TEACHING LEADERS TO ASK QUESTIONS THAT CAUSE TEAMS TO PRODUCE ANSWERS

Whether through speaking, authoring, or service on corporate and non-profit boards, Mark's passion for educating others is evident, and he spent eight years on the board of his alma mater's school of business. Institutions like MIT's Sloan School of Business, Northwestern's Kellogg School of Business, and RIT have invited him to talk with their students about his experiences with DBS and Lean in order to deepen their understanding of what does and doesn't add value.

Mark C. DeLuzio is a devoted family man and a Blue and Gold Star Father. He moved with his wife, Diane, from Connecticut to Arizona, so they didn't have to watch their grandchildren grow up on Facebook. Mark and Diane were instrumental in founding the Connecticut Trees of Honor Memorial Park, a serene space to reminisce and reflect as one walks the path of fallen military heroes (www.cttreesofhonor.com). Mark and Diane also formed B.R.A.V.E., a no-cost service that assists military veteran entrepreneurs in reaching their dreams with existing businesses or new start-ups (www.4thebrave.org).

1

Why Companies Have Flatlined

Seasoned executives are perplexed as to why their Lean efforts are now flatlining. These are the types of problems I'm seeing most often from talking with senior leaders in mature companies who seek my counsel:

- They do not understand that a Lean transformation is more than a cost reduction program.
- They typically view Lean as a manufacturing convention that does not apply to the rest of the business.
- They insist on running and structuring the organization with a traditional 1970s mindset.
- They believe that the fundamentals of Lean do not, or cannot, apply to their business.
- They've become confused by Lean consulting zealots promoting their latest product or service and tempted to move away from the basics of Lean.
- They fail to look at themselves critically when evaluating the reason for their "flatlined" performance.
- They are consistently being shown only one benchmark, Toyota, with little appreciation for the successes that "brownfield" companies have had in their journey toward excellence.

Sometimes it is hard to see something clearly when you are in the thick of it. As much as possible, it's going to be important to step back and try to examine your own leadership and what's happening in your company objectively. Aim to look for the root cause of why it is not working and divorce your ego from it.

In my consulting practice, I come upon organizations that are pretty mediocre when compared with world-class benchmarks. The problem is that they may still be making a lot of money or getting customer or industry kudos, so they see themselves as doing well and don't have much incentive to disrupt their processes and aim to be genuinely world class. You'll get the most value from this book when you can internalize that most organizations—and that probably includes yours, since you are wondering why it is flatlining on Lean —have a lot of room for improvement.

Ask yourself, "Do I want my company to be in the 98% or the 2%?"

Ninety-eight percent of all doctors, lawyers, and real estate agents are ones you don't want to deal with. There are only really 2% that are exceptional. This phenomenon applies to those companies who are involved with a Lean transformation. Very few actually realize the potential that is available and have the discipline to get into the 2%.

I liken the necessary discipline to that of a professional golfer versus a weekend golfer. A professional golfer has a regimented workout plan, several coaches for nutrition, putting, driving, irons, etc. We do not always attribute that level of discipline when running our business. We think we do, but we don't. A Lean transformation takes an incredible amount of discipline at all levels, yet few do this well in my experience.

This is also an example of how Lean is counterintuitive. You may be thinking, "But, getting to world class requires disruption and innovation, not discipline." The paradox of Lean is that the more structure and standards you have in place, the more flexible and creative you can become. Think of Lean as the string of buoys that keep swimmers in their lanes. They can do whatever they need to do to perform at their best, but if they depart from their lane, they will no longer be a contender in the race.

When Michael Phelps won 23 Olympic gold medals and 28 medals overall, did he stop trying to stay at world-class levels? He kept pushing to become better and better even though he was getting to be one of the oldest swimmers among his competitors. After his initial success, he went on to win more golds in subsequent Olympic games and held seven world records after the 2008 Olympics. He was a living model of continuous improvement.

Companies that are flatlining are clearly not disciplined about trying to get into the 2%. Or, if they have reached the 2%, they aren't aiming to be in the 1%. They aren't embracing the fact that world-class companies are always evolving and improving.

Now, let's dig deeper into why this happens. In our field experience over the past ten years, these are the four main reasons we've seen:

1. Lean is used as a short-term, tactical tool.
2. The Lean initiative isn't connected to the broader strategy.
3. Functions are optimized for Lean, but the enterprise isn't.
4. Leadership is either hands-off of Lean or reluctant to revisit its basics.

LEAN IS USED AS A SHORT-TERM, TACTICAL TOOL

I've found that many companies are using Lean for the sole purpose of getting results instead of to drive results-oriented processes that can be sustained. Focusing strictly on the results rather than the process which delivers the result is a very common mistake in a Lean transformation. This is especially true when companies are performing very well from a financial perspective.

Leaders in such companies become complacent and fail to create the burning platform within their organization to drive significant change. We saw this at Danaher. It took some coaxing for the more profitable divisions to realize that when they implemented Lean/DBS well, they became even more profitable in the long term. They had to make a culture shift to focus on the processes that would deliver world-class results rather than just on the results alone.

THE LEAN INITIATIVE ISN'T CONNECTED TO THE BROADER STRATEGY

Many of our Lean efforts were done for the sake of implementing Lean, without regard to our strategic initiatives. At times, we viewed the implementation of DBS/Lean as the business objective itself with little regard for quantitative business results backed by robust processes. We eventually learned that the tools of DBS were a means to achieve the objective, not the objective itself. It is common for companies new to Lean to get distracted from their business objectives, thereby spending valuable resources that will not move the needle. So, instead of transforming a significant value stream that will be meaningful to the customer, employees, and shareholders, companies sometimes tend to expend Lean resources to insignificant, non-strategic areas within the business.

CASE STUDY

When we implemented our first value stream at Danaher's Jake Brake in 1987, management wanted to transform a component process called the Auto-Lash line. The Auto-Lash was a small component that went into every Jake Brake that we produced, and consisted of three operators. Group Executive Art Byrne and Jake Brake President George Koenigsaecker wanted to make a bold statement internally that they were serious about the implementation of the Toyota Production System, but we would not be catching anyone's attention by focusing on the Auto-Lash line. Additionally, there would be little benefit realized in terms of safety, quality, delivery, and cost. So Art and George decided to transform the Caterpillar machining and assembly line. The Caterpillar business represented approximately 33% of Jake's revenue, so the risks were high, but the opportunity to underscore the commitment behind implementing TPS was in keeping with their vision of changing the culture. Looking back, we made some fundamental mistakes, but it was a huge success overall. Although we didn't realize it at the time, we were on the doorstep of making history by launching the modern Lean movement in the United States.

Lean alone can help you grow your business and provide a competitive advantage, but these gains will be short-lived when they are not backed with strategy. A company that excels with Lean but makes cement life preservers will not succeed, regardless of how robust their Lean transformation. Take a look at Delphi. They have been the recipients of many Lean awards such as the Shingo Prize. However, their strategy was not aligned to address the challenges that were eventually the demise of that business. We have found that 70% of your kaizen efforts should be focused toward your strategic breakthrough objectives as outlined in strategy deployment. The remaining 30% should be dedicated to daily management. You'll find more detail on strategy deployment and daily management in Chapter 5.

FUNCTIONS ARE OPTIMIZED FOR LEAN, BUT THE ENTERPRISE ISN'T

For Lean to realize lasting results for the entire company, it must be radiated across the enterprise. It can't just exist in manufacturing, yet it often does.

CASE STUDY

I was once contacted by the CEO of a specialty valve manufacturer who wanted us to implement Lean on the shop floor. The shop floor consisted of several large CNC machining centers and assembly operations. He indicated to me that they were having trouble meeting their delivery commitments to customers, and he believed the root cause of this was their productivity issues on the shop floor.

I suggested to the CEO that we perform an end-to-end value stream map of the operations. He agreed, and our value stream analysis discovered that his product had a 60-day lead time, with a total process time of only 15 hours. It was further discovered that of the 60-day lead time, 45 days we attributed to the front-end, engineered-to-order configuration department. In fact, approximately 80% of the orders sent to the shop floor were already past the confirmed delivery date with the customer.

Instead of focusing our initial attention on the shop floor, we concentrated on the order configuration process. Through careful analysis and subsequent improvements, we were able to reduce the lead time for this process from 45 days to just 5 days over the course of five months. We eventually turned our attention to the shop floor opportunities, but not until we fixed the order configuration process, which was an obvious priority once we identified it as so through the use of value stream mapping.

This example shows the tendency to focus one's entire Lean efforts to the shop floor. However, many of the problems found on the shop floor resonate from other areas of the organization. For example, quality defects are often traced to an ineffective product development process. On-time delivery issues, as just illustrated, can be traced to an ineffective demand management process.

Most Lean initiatives start by attempting to improve a single function or targeted area. We call these point kaizens. Point kaizens are easier to do than enterprise-wide kaizens and they result in quick wins rather than sustainable results. It's no wonder that when the initial wave of point kaizens is complete, companies will "flatline" in their operating results.

LEADERSHIP IS EITHER HANDS-OFF OF LEAN OR RELUCTANT TO REVISIT ITS BASICS

Probably the most frequent reason we see for flatlining is that leaders are not owning the problem. They know the company has a problem, but they don't think they have anything to do with it. Some variation of, "I'm okay, but everyone else is screwed up," is what I hear all the time. Leaders must be willing to examine their own knowledge of the basics of Lean and how they manage these, as well as become active participants in a Lean transformation.

I recently began working with a multibillion-dollar diversified manufacturing company that has been implementing Lean in their plant for the past ten years and now they've flatlined. They are still using MRP (manufacturing requirements planning), a batch-and-queue-driven push system. They don't have pull or flow systems or standard work and are only doing one to two kaizens a month. Their reasons are that they are "high mix/low volume" and that Lean concepts do not apply to their business. Little did they know, that condition is exactly the one in which Toyota Production System principles were developed. This client had to be willing to stop insisting on doing the same things and thinking in the same old ways.

You'll see in Chapter 4 why kaizen, standard work, etc. are all critical to a sustainable Lean initiative. Because they hit a wall with their Lean transformation, this client had to revisit these fundamentals.

Lean leaders often treat Lean as a spectator sport that they can manage from the sidelines. In reality, Lean requires experiential knowledge. Leaders can't think, "I've reached a certain level of seniority and the basics are for those in the trenches, not the corner office." You can't achieve kaizen (continuous improvement) without getting actively involved in the organization's transformation.

2

The Solution in Five Steps

Now that you have insight into why your organization has been flatlining on Lean and why it's important to shift your approach, I want to introduce you to the steps that will allow you to breathe new life into your Lean initiatives and achieve sustained results.

Unlike some books where a method is only tested in one company, these steps were derived from my unique experience across hundreds of Lean transformations. Through these interactions, I've noticed common themes to what was effective in reviving an occurrence of flatlining, which I distilled into five steps.

The five steps, with an entire chapter in this book devoted to each one, are:

1. Shift your Lean mindset for sustainable results.
2. Default to the basics.
3. Align your Lean transformation with strategy.
4. Make Lean an enterprise endeavor.
5. Use Lean principles to evolve your company's culture.

SHIFT YOUR LEAN MINDSET FOR SUSTAINABLE RESULTS

I've come across many leaders who've convinced themselves that their business requires a different kind of approach. Yet, Lean principles apply regardless of what kind of business you are in. As I mentioned, for almost three decades, I've worked with client companies in oil and gas, automotive, aerospace, insurance, financial services, pharmaceutical and many other industries.

Lean requires a counterintuitive way of thinking because traditional practices aren't conducive to Lean. We may have learned things in business school or from our work in industry that we accept as "right." For example, it's ingrained in our brain that getting as much product out of a machine as possible is a good use of capital. When you read Chapter 4, you'll understand why this may not be such a wise objective.

Do you really need to be producing a little bag of plastic parts for the assembly process, or could you just put those parts right at the point of use, eliminating bagging and stockroom operations altogether? We accept that machined parts need to be deburred, but we don't think of that rework process as wasteful. What if you were to just manufacture a conforming part in the first place to eliminate the need for deburring? Why do accountants need to reconcile a set of numbers? If the source data were correct to begin with, there wouldn't be a need for reconciling. These examples may seem obvious, but most don't see the waste in them because they aren't questioning the "baked-in" practices that they may have inherited.

Or, maybe you are already highly focused on efficiencies, but not thinking about the customer. In Chapter 3, I explain what I call the Lean Trilogy and how the three primary stakeholders—customer, employee, and shareholder—all have to be considered when building lasting transformations.

Most importantly, I want you to start thinking of Lean as a growth vehicle for your entire organization rather than just a tool for addressing cost-cutting initiatives.

Are you ready to unlearn a lot of what you were taught?

DEFAULT TO THE BASICS

"Basics" are the tenets of Lean that must be adopted and implemented for you to be practicing Lean. If your organization is flatlining on Lean and you aren't really doing Lean correctly or completely, the basics covered in Chapter 4 will get you back on track. These include Heijunka level scheduling, standard work, kaizen, just in time, jidoka, and the SQDC hierarchy. I will discuss and compare the way we live our personal lives with how we conduct ourselves when running our businesses. In general, most of us are very good at living our personal lives in accordance with Lean principles. When it comes to running our businesses, we tend to divert from these principles, which in turn prevent us from realizing our true potential.

Often leaders want to avoid the basics because they may take some relearning, plus they aren't easy to master. Initially, it may seem as if the Lean basics are in conflict with traditional, comfortable business practices. They are! But you'll want to stay the course and orient toward these proven tenets. The Lean basics are not exciting but they will get you further faster, and that will make you look better at the end of the day than if you had tried to introduce the next "silver bullet."

ALIGN YOUR LEAN TRANSFORMATION WITH STRATEGY

Lean and strategy go hand in hand. Some leading thinkers in the Lean world view *Lean as a strategy*. I agree, but with a caveat. Lean is not a strategy in itself and does not replace the need for a good *business* strategy. Instead, it's a competitive weapon that will help you *execute* a good strategy.

I believe that a business strategy should not be only an annual event, but also an ongoing business process that's incorporated just like any other Lean tool. A good business strategy should concisely describe the few things that a company must do to profitably grow in the marketplace.

Strategy is implemented by using strategy deployment (described in Chapter 5), sometimes called policy deployment, Hoshin Kanri, or Hoshin planning. Strategy deployment is the means for converting strategy into reality. It's an integrated and disciplined process to align breakthrough performance improvements with the necessary organizational resources. It is a key to preventing strategic planning documents from being shelved once formulated and agreed. Strategy deployment funnels strategic business objectives into tangible processes and multifunctional teams that need to be improved or, in many cases, developed.

MAKE LEAN AN ENTERPRISE ENDEAVOR

Most Lean transformations initially start by implementing "point" kaizen. Point kaizen typically focuses on a single process within a function of the organization. An example would be creating a one-piece flow manufacturing cell with accompanying standard work, 5S, visual controls, etc. However, if an organization never graduates to "enterprise" kaizen, they will never self-actualize as a benchmark company.

To achieve a successful, full-enterprise Lean transformation, an organization must have the maturity to engage in kaizen that centers on how the enterprise is structured and operates. In other words, it must involve all functions of an organization and requires advanced understanding of Lean by the CEO and functional leaders, as well as a willingness to move away from traditional business practices.

In Chapter 6, I also cover:

- Why value stream management is the key to having functions organized in ways that align with Lean principles and better serve the customer. It's not just about changing processes within a given function or department.
- How mura and muri are the forms of waste that are typically generated by leadership policies and rarely get addressed.
- What it is about traditional cost accounting systems that drive behavior that goes against the grain of Lean thinking.

USE LEAN PRINCIPLES TO EVOLVE YOUR COMPANY'S CULTURE

The focus of Lean is typically on the tools themselves. I like to use the analogy that if I know how to use a saw, drill, hammer, etc., that doesn't mean I know how to build a house. A Lean transformation is the same. You must go beyond using the tools for improvements to applying Lean's principles in ways that they become indoctrinated into your business thinking and culture to impact the organization as a whole.

While there is a lot we can emulate from Toyota, there is a difference between becoming like Toyota or becoming Toyota-like. You can understand the principles of Lean, and still fail at implementing Lean. When you are dealing with real people in a place that already has established ways of doing things, it's about evolution rather than building from the ground up. To be able to challenge the status quo, you'll need to have the right Lean leadership in place.

We learned the hard way at Danaher that high-potential leaders who are 100% dedicated to Lean have to be appointed to key Lean positions throughout the organization. Initially, our leadership assigned the least qualified, most expendable person to head up DBS—evidence that they didn't have confidence in it. Additionally, many divisions gave their local DBS representative other line responsibilities in addition to their DBS role. For example, at one location, the DBS representative was also the Quality and Engineering Manager. We learned that their line responsibilities always took precedent over implementing Lean.

In Chapter 7, I expand on the competencies Lean leaders should have to be able to evolve the culture effectively, including knowing how to deal with naysayers, delegate problem-solving, and not be satisfied with the status quo. In this book's addendum, I included the agenda for our Lean Leadership Bootcamp.

Now, let's jump in to the first of the five steps that prevent flatlining with Lean.

3

Step 1

Shift the Lean Mindset for Sustainable Results

I have heard varying reasons as to why companies are undertaking a Lean initiative. Some want to do it because it will look good in their annual report. Others want to reduce costs or need to improve quality, service, and lead time issues. Very few, however, have the vision that Lean can drive profitable growth or understand the culture change that will be needed to be successful. Most of these companies initiate a Lean transformation simply with the shareholder in mind, giving little, if any, consideration to other stakeholders.

To achieve sustainable results over the long term with Lean, a mindset shift must happen in these four areas:

- Lean as a trilogy;
- "we're different" mentality;
- Lean as a growth vehicle;
- the Six Sigma hysteria.

THE LEAN TRILOGY

The first mindset shift for lasting results to be achieved is to consider the equilibrium among the stakeholders in the Lean Trilogy: the employee, the customer, and the shareholder (Figure 3.1). There are other stakeholders, such as suppliers and society-at-large, but if you

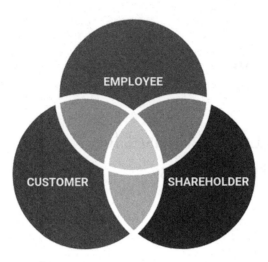

FIGURE 3.1 The Lean Trilogy

don't meet the requirements of these primary ones, the Lean transformation will fail.

Many Lean initiatives commence with just the shareholder in mind. For example, if you are using Lean to reduce headcount, shareholders profit because expenses are cut. The employees lose in this situation. One group cannot benefit at the expense of another because Lean should not be a zero-sum game. When only one stakeholder is winning, you may see temporary gains, but you've compromised the long-term viability of your Lean transformation.

I recently spoke with the Lean person-in-charge at a large financial institution that started a transformation quite a few years ago. Let's call him Jeff. Following a failed cost-cutting attempt, Jeff wanted my perspective on their path forward. He essentially disclosed that the focus of their Lean transformation was to take costs out of the business, thereby improving profitability. As I listened to him describe their situation, Jeff used the word "cost" over a dozen times as the primary objective. Never once did he mention their customers or employees. Further reinforcing their cost-only mindset, Jeff reported directly to the chief financial officer.

As we talked, I learned that their CEO's primary objective was satisfying the shareholders through cost-cutting, and Jeff was looking for someone to lead this transformation anew, reporting to him. I told Jeff that they already have the person in place that should guide the transformation, the CEO. He insisted that the CEO is already committed. I asked,

"Who wouldn't be supportive of lower operating costs? Is your CEO and leadership team willing to satisfy other stakeholders, namely customers and employees?" Jeff responded, "Well, of course." I had my doubts.

Let's take a look at the three stakeholder groups.

1 Employees

Many seasoned Lean practitioners I've encountered do not fully comprehend that a Lean transformation is all about people. Instead, they view Lean as a set of tools and methodologies. To gain employee buy-in and support, it's crucial to understand their "What's In It For Me?" (WIFM) factor. Employees' attitude toward their superiors, company, customers, and work need to be a positive force that's aligned with the goals of the organization.

The rate of change in the continuous improvement (CI) process does have an impact on people. It has the potential to motivate or demotivate. As they are going through the learning process, employees will oscillate between effective and ineffective. Leaders must have tolerance for allowing employees to make mistakes, always focusing on the process and not the individual. There's an understanding that people are generally oriented toward wanting to do a good job.

Refer to Figure 3.2. As leaders, we want all of our people to be in the ME quadrant. As employees continue to make positive change, they will

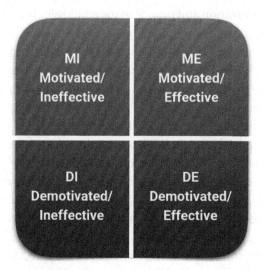

FIGURE 3.2 The Motivation Model

oscillate between ME and MI. Leadership must provide air cover and encourage, recognize, and reward those employees with the will to make positive change. Ineffective employees must be given the proper training to succeed.

Employees in the DI quadrant need to either change or leave the organization. You will find DI employees at all levels of the organization, from the C-suite to the support staff. It has been our experience that these naysayers represent about 10% of the organization. Employees in the DE sector need coaching to get them motivated. Studies prove that the more employees are involved in kaizen events, the more satisfied they are with their jobs.

CASE STUDY

A VP of a mid-sized manufacturing company attended a kaizen report-out on a Friday afternoon. The team felt they made great progress all week; however, the VP second-guessed them, saying they should've done this and that. The team was utterly demoralized. Subsequent kaizen events were not met with the level of enthusiasm required to change the organization significantly. This VP eventually failed at his job and was replaced.

Working in an environment where problems are minimized has a direct impact on the motivation and morale of the employee. Therefore, processes must be designed that allow employees at all levels to succeed in meeting the organization's operating and financial objectives. A well-thought-out process shouldn't have any errors. If organizations put as much focus and effort into developing these processes as they do in obtaining top talent or procuring a piece of equipment, they would achieve lasting results.

The joke in the marketplace is that LEAN means Less Employees Are Needed. It is a mistake to tie headcount reductions to the Lean process. After all, how can you ask for employees' ideas and then lay them off when they "kaizen" themselves out of a job? How much success could you have with future kaizen efforts? When a kaizen team finds a genuine need to reduce the headcount required for a particular work area, what should happen to the employees? Having a game plan in advance is crucial.

Some forward-thinking executives, like Art Byrne, former CEO of Wiremold, had a "no layoff" policy as a result of Lean improvements. He

opted to reassign and retrain workers, insource where possible, and place excess headcount on kaizen improvement teams. Of course, as there was attrition, those employees did not need to be replaced unless needed to support rapid growth. Because they were also smartly thinking of Lean as a growth strategy—and their sales force could leverage this operating excellence—the headcount took care of itself as the company profitably grew. Art led one of the most successful Lean transformations in US history while at Wiremold.

2 Customers

Even though we've been acclimated to the concept of "voice of the customer," companies often believe they know how to satisfy the customer without ever asking what is important to them.

CASE STUDY

In my early days as a general manager of the Asian Business of Jake Brake, my team was delivering 100% on-time delivery with 100% quality. When I went to Japan, I expected my customer to give me accolades for such excellent performance. Upon our visit, we were told that we ranked 106th out of 110 suppliers. What we didn't realize was that we were being graded on our responsiveness to their various inquiries and requests. Because of the 12-hour time difference between the east coast and Asia, we were always delinquent. We quickly learned not to assume we knew what is important to the customer and to ask instead.

In keeping the balance in the Lean Trilogy, you can't keep customers happy at the expense of employees and shareholders. Customers would love for you to cut prices in half. However, shareholders and employees would be impacted by lost profits and closed plants. In balancing the customer equation, it's also important to understand the value they bring to your business. There are good groups of customers and bad ones. Customers who have unrealistic expectations or fail to operate ethically could cost you money. If employee and/or shareholder requirements aren't met, you may need to decide not to do business with certain customers.

3 Shareholders

I have worked with many clients who only consider the shareholder objectives in their decision-making process. Actions to satisfy your employees and customers are usually the drivers that will deliver satisfactory results to shareholders. Keep in mind that as we drive to optimize all three stakeholder groups, tradeoffs at times will be necessary.

For example, with the 2018 tax revision, many companies handed out employee bonuses, which seems in direct conflict with shareholder interests. Short-term thinking would look at this bonus as a mere cost that impacts profits and stock growth. However, strategic shareholders can favor the long-term value of fostering goodwill among employees and a climate geared toward employee retention—which ultimately costs less than employee turnover.

In the final analysis, the long-term success of a company's Lean transformation is maximized by satisfying the needs of all three stakeholder groups. Keep in mind that any one decision isn't always going to satisfy all three constituencies. Aim for striking a balance by considering the benefits for each over an arc of time. Strategic plans need to address these areas, and leadership must be prepared to measure their success objectively. Additionally, a formal feedback process must be in place to monitor the company's success in terms of employees, customers, and shareholders.

THE "WE'RE DIFFERENT" MENTALITY

Almost every type of business I work with considers themselves "different." They may be, but this is not a reason for them to reject the Lean methodology as it applies to their organization. Many times, executives get confused by attempting to relate the Lean tools and Toyota to their business. What they need to do is to elevate their thinking and understand how Lean *principles* do apply to their business.

One of the key assumptions Lean makes is that there is waste in every business and business process. Lean's kaizen philosophy is that we will always try to improve with the ultimate goal of achieving perfection (which, by definition, we will never achieve). So, executives need to incorporate Lean principles as well as tools to identify and eliminate the waste that resides within their business.

CASE STUDY

In my initial meeting with the president of a newly acquired acquisition at Danaher, he proceeded to tell me that the Danaher Business System (DBS) did not apply to his company ... that they were "different." I told him: "Yes, you are different... You are making 4% operating profit, and the average Danaher company is earning 17%. You are turning inventory 2x, and the average Danaher company is at 20x. Your on-time delivery performance is 45%, and the average Danaher company is 95%." I agreed he was different and that if he continued to have his "we're different" mentality, he would need to find a "different" job. He soon thereafter understood these benchmarks and fully adopted DBS. His turnaround was a complete success.

Typically, I have found the "we're different" mentality amongst executives is a cover for resisting change. I once had an executive who manufactured wrenches say out loud that his business is not like Toyota, that he doesn't make cars. So, I asked, do you think making wrenches is as complicated as making cars? He replied: "No, I think it is MORE difficult!" He clearly did not want to buy in and was soon replaced due to his unwillingness to change.

Some of the "we're different" mentality is normal in the beginning, but if executives continue to insist that they are different after being educated on Lean, it is usually a telltale sign that they are not going to buy into their Lean transformation.

LEAN AS A GROWTH VEHICLE

The prevailing paradigm that exists today is that Lean is about reducing costs. Lean is also sometimes limited to the manufacturing realm. The next mindset shift in optimizing your Lean transformation is to understand that Lean can be used to drive growth across the enterprise in all types of industries.

How Is Lean an Enterprise Growth Strategy?

When companies use Lean to improve customer experience in terms of quality, lead times, on-time delivery, and overall service, it results in a sustainable competitive advantage versus their competition. This advantage results in business growth.

Conversely, losing focus on operating metrics often creates declining sales revenue or prohibits entry into new customers or markets. I have witnessed many companies who have lost market share simply by allowing their core operating metrics (quality, on-time delivery, lead time) to deteriorate. Additionally, I have seen companies unable to enter more competitive markets with higher standards, such as the Japanese market, simply because their operating markets were not competitive.

The maniacal focus on cost alone has derailed many improvement initiatives. Changing one's perspective is necessary. Instead of viewing:

- quality as a cost, think of the lost revenues due to poor quality;
- headcount as a cost, ask yourself if the process is fully documented with standard work and if employees are trained to this standard;
- lead time as a cost, think of increasing process flexibility, therefore allowing the company to react quickly to schedule changes and customer requests and use lead time advantages over the competition to win business.

You will get the most growth mileage out of your Lean transformation when you leverage the newfound capabilities (quality, lead time, etc.) in the value proposition your sales force is bringing to the marketplace. Especially in a commodity business, where quality and service performance are the only differentiators, these changes must be intentionally communicated, both throughout the organization and to the customer base. With these newfound capabilities, it allows the sales team to shift the discussion from price to value-adding services and capabilities.

By incorporating Lean as a growth strategy, companies can make the mistake of only benchmarking against their competition when they really need to benchmark against world-class standards. In other words, just because you have the best quality in your industry doesn't mean that you are a quality company. I cover world-class benchmarking in Chapter 5.

THE SIX SIGMA HYSTERIA

One also needs to change their mindset about *partially* adopting Lean as the solution. I've found this is harder for companies to do when they've also jumped on the Six Sigma bandwagon (or any of the other tools that get confused with Lean). When Jack Welch mandated Six Sigma as *the* improvement vehicle for GE, he closed off other ideas for continuous improvement and paved the way for thousands of copycat companies to spend millions of dollars on Six Sigma initiatives requiring highly paid consultants. Wanting to capitalize on this trend, consulting firms sold Six Sigma as the be-all and end-all of business improvement tools rather than being true to what Six Sigma is meant to address. Many company leaders excitedly bought into the opportunity to introduce something new.

Even though Six Sigma was being seen as the replacement for Lean, my high-level contacts at GE were still secretly implementing Lean manufacturing methodologies, fearfully hiding their "treasonous" efforts from senior leadership. Eventually, the business world became confused over the difference between Lean and Six Sigma. To appease both camps, the term Lean Six Sigma was born, further unsettling the marketplace—yet, opening a new path for more consultants to sell their wares.

It's important to understand that Lean is not Six Sigma. Six Sigma is a statistical problem-solving process that fits under the Lean umbrella. Rather than competing with Lean, it should sit alongside all of the other tools in the Lean toolbox.

The majority of companies that have relied on the Six Sigma approach have failed to increase shareholder value. More than a decade ago, Charles Holland of Qualpro did a study finding that 91% of the 58 companies that had announced Six Sigma programs trailed the S&P 500. Even Jack Welch has conceded that Six Sigma shouldn't be used in every corner of the organization. We are all aware that GE has fallen from the graces of the elite companies, evidenced by poor performance and their dismissal from the Dow Jones Industrial Index.

Let's look at the reasons why Six Sigma hasn't been the cure-all it was purported to be.

1 It's the Wrong Tool for the Job

Six Sigma and Lean are both attempts to make improvement and solve problems. Six Sigma is a set of statistical problem-solving tools that follow a model of define, measure, analyze, improve, and control. Lean follows the Deming cycle: the plan, do, check, act model. On the surface, using Six Sigma to improve quality and reduce variation seems reasonable. The issue has become an over-reliance on Six Sigma to solve problems that other approaches would be better at addressing. The adage applies that when the only tool in your toolbox is a hammer, all of your problems look like nails.

While Six Sigma has its place in the continuous improvement spectrum, I have seen it applied to inappropriate situations. When we worked on our benchmark kaizen at GE's Money division, we applied Lean to their process and reduced their lead time from 63 days to 1 day. The process time to accomplish the amount of work necessary to complete one order was just one hour. The Six Sigma engineers had been trying to reduce the process time from one hour without any consideration for the 63-day lead time inherent in the process. This was a misuse of the tool and, quite frankly, the wrong one for this task. We used traditional value stream mapping and other Lean approaches to reduce the lead time, which resulted in $216 million of additional revenue in the first year alone. This breakthrough was noticed by senior GE leadership, including CEO Jeff Immelt, and gave rise to the popularity of Lean methodologies within General Electric.

For one of our clients, there was a specific application where Six Sigma would have made sense. Their foundry process had over 25 variables that needed to be set correctly in order to assure a quality part. So, a Six Sigma tool called design of experiments (DOE) was the right tool of choice. However, the VP of Corporate Quality wanted to institute Six Sigma across the entire company, which would have negatively impacted initiatives that were better suited to Lean.

The bottom line is that 90% of the problems most businesses face can be solved with Lean because it offers a broader range of tools to address various situations. Companies should not ever try to merge Lean and Six Sigma together as this derails Lean efforts. Use Six Sigma strategically for specific problems. Do not try to create an entire culture around a tool such as Six Sigma, as many companies have attempted. So, when your quality assurance lead decides to introduce Six Sigma to optimize everything in the plant, be aware that this is likely not the best use of resources and that Lean is more efficient and effective.

2 It Takes Longer

Six Sigma demands a more significant time investment because:

- It requires upfront, expensive training and improvements cannot commence until proper certification at various levels is achieved (master black belt, black belt, green belt, etc.). On the other hand, improvements can start immediately with Lean.
- It tends to look at comprehensive solutions to address all situations, which adds lead time before the improvement process can even begin.
- Each project requires significant, time-consuming data collection and analysis.
- Six Sigma projects average several months, while the typical Lean kaizen initiative achieves results in a matter of days. The continuous improvement nature of Lean has an inherent sense of urgency. Also, the spirit of the kaizen process looks for a 70–75% solution instead of trying to address every nuance. "Don't let perfect get in the way of better" is what Lean practitioners need to keep in mind.

3 Six Sigma Has a Goal of 3.4 Defects per Million

One of my Japanese senseis lectured me that Six Sigma is "no good!!" He said that we should have a mindset of zero defects, not 3.4 per million! If airlines targeted a 3.4 per million quality rating regarding safe flights, there would be an airline crash somewhere in the world every three days. Clearly, there are specific industries, such as aviation, where defects are unacceptable. Yet, all companies that aim to be world class should strive for this. You may be thinking, "But, achieving zero defects would be cost-prohibitive." Studies show that the cost of poor quality (COPQ) ranges anywhere from 15–25% of a firm's revenues. The cost of rework, delays, scrapped product, inspection warranty, liability, lost business, etc., make it difficult to argue that zero defects should not be the goal. Look to Lean for the total elimination of defects.

We know that one of the Lean principles is that you should always assure quality of the part or service before passing it on to the next process. However, Six Sigma relies on a statistical process called SPC (statistical process control). SPC violates this principle. Let's say you wanted to take measurements of the inner diameter of a bore. With SPC, you may check one out of every fifteen parts. My Japanese sensei, Mr. Iwata, told us: "If you are going to check one, check them all. Would you want an airline to check one out of fifteen airplanes?" He couldn't understand why 14 out of 15 parts were not checked, and if the 15th part passed inspection, the other 14 parts would be passed to the next process without having been quality-assured. If you aren't assuring quality through process and product design, inspection is a must to avoid violating the principle of unknowingly passing a part on to the next process without first assuring its quality.

4 It's Not Inclusive

I asked a Six Sigma leader how he engaged his workforce in the improvement process, and he said, "Employees are instructed to fill out a check sheet to record quality measurements." Nowhere were employees asked to contribute their ideas as to how to improve the quality of the product or process. Since a company cannot afford to put all of their employees through Six Sigma training, very few can engage in the process beyond basic data collection.

Lean, on the other hand, allows employees to contribute their ideas immediately in the continuous improvement process. Employees at all levels can play a significant role in making and implementing their recommendations. In fact, your best consultants are the employees who are executing the work on a day-to-day basis. Even though they are intimately familiar with the work, many times they are not asked to contribute their ideas.

CASE STUDY

A UK firm that produced temperature controllers had false readings on their test equipment. Product that was later proven to be "good product" was being recorded as failures. To determine the root of the problem, I facilitated a CEDAC (cause and effect diagram with the addition of cards) exercise. While we were exploring potential causes, an employee offered that the problem only happens on weekdays, not weekends. This one piece of data led us to find that the factory adjacent to the plant never worked weekends, only weekdays. Upon further investigation, we found that the nearby factory emitted electronic magnetic interference (EMI) from its manufacturing process, and this was interfering with the test stands. The solution was to shroud the test stands with an insulating material to prevent readings from being affected by the EMI. This problem would never have been detected by a Six Sigma engineer without this kind of employee input.

While there is a lot to learn in both Lean and Six Sigma methodologies, Six Sigma is far more technical and excludes those without a proper statistical background.

5 Elimination of Wasteful Processes vs. Improving Wasteful Processes

It's been my experience that many Six Sigma improvement initiatives were conducted on processes that Lean would attempt to eliminate because they should not have existed in the first place. Lean continually asks: "Am I doing things right, or am I doing the right things?"

SUMMARY

Many of the suggestions in this chapter address the mindset of leadership and the misnomers related to Lean transformations. It also places high value on leaders getting the proper education so that they can lead the organization in accordance with the Lean philosophy and avoid taking their organizations down the wrong path. I've found that the leaders who can keep these concepts in mind are equipped to prevent or correct flatlining in their Lean transformation.

QUESTIONS TO ASK

At the end of each of the "Five Steps" chapters, you'll find a set of questions that I feel are important to answer. They may seem basic; however, it's the basic questions that usually lead us to the highest value. To yield a higher-quality Lean transformation, I encourage you and your leadership team to discuss these questions in an open forum:

- Have you considered all of your stakeholders and what is important to them?
- Have you set measurable goals that are important to these stakeholders?
- Do you truly understand the way your customers measure you as a supplier of goods and services?
- Do you think that your business is so unique that the principles of Lean do not apply to you?
- Do you use your Lean capabilities (better quality, shorter lead times, outstanding on-time delivery) in the value-selling process with your customers?
- Do you view Lean as a cost-cutting measure or as a profitable growth vehicle?
- Are you confusing your organization with the melding of Lean and Six Sigma?

4

Step 2

Default to the Basics

Why is it important to default to the basics?

The Toyota Production System model (represented in Figure 4.1), which evolved into the modern version of Lean, is built on a foundation of:

- Heijunka-level scheduling;
- standard work;
- kaizen.

And then there are the two pillars: just in time (JIT) and jidoka.

Without these foundational elements—considered the basics of Lean—one is practicing "fake Lean."

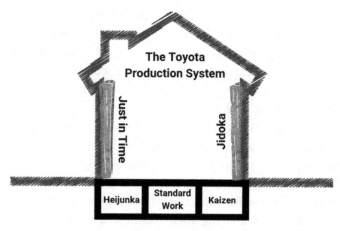

FIGURE 4.1 Ohno's Toyota Production System Model

Frequently, I visit companies who proclaim to be "doing Lean;" however, they are not applying Heijunka, standard work, or kaizen. I recently went into one company that had visual evidence of doing a good job with Lean from sign boards to posters to yellow tape on the shop floor. However, they were using a push manufacturing system, didn't have standard work in place, and were doing very few kaizen activities. They were a model of "fake Lean."

You can't just do the easy parts of Lean or create window dressing around it and expect to generate the desired results. This is like a body-builder who wishes to become Mr. Universe but who isn't willing to lift weights. Often, what is essential for success isn't easy.

In the rest of this chapter, I'll detail why each of these basics are critical to preventing your Lean initiative from flatlining:

- Heijunka level scheduling, standard work, and kaizen;
- just in time and jidoka;
- the SQDC hierarchy;
- relate back to real life.

HEIJUNKA LEVEL SCHEDULING

Heijunka is a process to level-load the production schedule over a predetermined time horizon. Because it's difficult and disruptive to manage a process where volume severely fluctuates on a day-to-day basis, Heijunka combats this by specifying the amount of inventory that must be produced in a given time period. Many assume that Heijunka only applies to a manufacturing operation; however, it is applicable to an administrative process as well. For example, an insurance company that processes claims will be more efficient and easier to manage if it had a level-loaded "production" schedule of claims.

For this to be effective, it is paramount that all functions of the organization collaborate to achieve this goal. This is usually done through a sales and operations planning process (S&OP) that gets critical input from sales, marketing, finance, engineering, human resources, and operations. My experience is that most companies do not optimize this process since they insist on managing their business from a siloed functional perspective, not an enterprise perspective. I have observed on many occasions the manufacturing operations' attempt to unilaterally level their production schedule without input from other functions. They all inevitably fail. Most organizations place a high value on obtaining functional goals and objectives; however, in the Lean world, it is crucial that they work together in order to optimize the entire enterprise. I cover why it's necessary to manage Lean transformations from an enterprise point of view in Chapter 6.

To further facilitate a successful Heijunka level scheduling system, the concepts of flow and pull must be mastered. Flow is the continuous movement of product from one process to the next, without stopping to be stockpiled. This may be simple to conceptualize, but in practice it is one of the most difficult things to do in Lean. Underlying this concept is the idea of a customer order generating the demand for a product produced in a flow environment. So, each product that is produced is correlated with customer demand.

The opposite of flow is "push," where product is made in batches without regard for customer demand. Product produced in the push fashion usually ends up as stockpiles of inventory on the shop floor or in a warehouse. Lean teaches us that we should never use "push" as a production system. If I were called in to give the stamp of approval on a Lean plan, I couldn't do it if it incorporated any form of a push system.

What if it is not possible to flow product? Because we don't want to push a product, we need a middle ground. That middle ground is called "pull." Pull is usually achieved by creating a kanban system, an inventory control system that keeps the minimum amount of inventory necessary at various locations where flow is not possible.

People new to Lean tend to establish kanban in areas that would be better served by a flow system. One of my Japanese mentors, Mr. Chiro Nakao, gave us some food for thought concerning kanban pull systems. He said, "Kanban is an admission of failure to do one-piece flow." With that thought in mind, he was challenging us to make the improvements to our manufacturing system where kanban wouldn't be needed at all. Most novices to Lean think that kanbans are normal ... our sensei taught us that kanbans are abnormal, and that we should always strive to achieve flow.

Note that there are other forms of "pull" systems, such as flow lanes, but this is beyond the scope of this book. Suffice it to say that the order of preference in Lean is to flow where you can, pull where you can't flow, and never, ever push.

STANDARD WORK

Standard work is a tool that defines the interaction of people and their environment when processing a repetitive product or service. To provide a routine for consistency of the operation, it specifies the motion of the operator and the sequence of action. Having a habit for repetitive tasks makes managing them (scheduling, resource allocation) easier. Similar to Heijunka, standard work applies to repetitive administrative processes, as well as manufacturing processes.

By detailing the one "best way/process" we currently know and understand, it also highlights what is normal and abnormal—preventing backsliding and giving the necessary standard, or basis, for improvement. With the continuous improvement mantra, "tomorrow it should be better," the standard work should be revised to incorporate future improvements.

Many companies create manufacturing cells through the rearrangement of equipment, but fail to institute standard work. This is analogous to an orchestra playing a concert without sheet music!

Standard work has three central elements:

1. takt time;
2. standard work sequence;
3. standard work in process.

1 Takt Time

Takt is a German word meaning beat or rhythm, and it's the rate that a customer is placing orders on a particular operation. It is defined by taking the available time during a production shift (usually expressed in seconds) and dividing it by the customer demand for that particular shift. For example, if there were 27,000 seconds available in a shift with a daily demand of 270 units, the takt time would equate to 100 seconds. What does this mean? It means that if you were to stand at the end of a production line, one good part should fall off the line every 100 seconds. **Not** 90 seconds, **not** 110 seconds! If you produced too fast at 90 seconds, you would build unnecessary inventory. If you produced at 110 seconds, you would miss customer delivery commitments or put yourself into an overtime situation. It also means that in a one-piece flow environment, an operator cannot have more than 100 seconds of cycle time for their respective operations within their standard work sequence. Likewise, the processing cycle time of a piece of equipment cannot exceed the takt time of 100 seconds, otherwise you will have a bottleneck and your drop-off rate will exceed the 100-second takt time.

CASE STUDY

I received a call from a client where a newly formed manufacturing cell was not getting the desired daily production output, despite the fact that they had instituted standard work. They were looking to produce 40 units per day, and they were only achieving 35 units. I flew to Cleveland to investigate, and the first question I asked was: "What's the takt time?" Their takt time was 675 seconds. The very next thing I did was a time study of all seven operators in the cell. Six of the seven operators' cycle times were at or slightly below takt time. However, one of the operators was timed at 770 seconds, considerably over takt. Coincidently, if you divide 27,000 available seconds by 770 seconds, the result is 35! That one operator was the bottleneck and limited the drop-off rate of the cell to 35 units per day. We evaluated the respective work sequences of all seven operators, reassigned operations within their respective work sequence, reduced the cycle time through kaizen activities, and assured that all operators were operating within the stated takt time. They successfully achieved 40 units per day.

It is important to note in the case study above that it was not the operator's fault for exceeding takt time. This was simply a process issue and the incorrect amount of work was assigned to her. In Lean, we have a saying: "Don't blame the person, blame the process." Most employees want to do a good job, and we can assume that this particular operator was working excessively to keep up with the others in the cell. Traditional managers would first look to blame the operator as opposed to analyzing the process. Standard work should not be used as a disciplinary tool, but as a tool for continuous improvement.

Takt time is a powerful tool and can be used in any repetitive process, whether it is a manufacturing or administrative process. Running a process without takt time is analogous to an orchestra playing without a conductor.

2 Standard Work Sequence

Standard work sequence defines the series of operations an operator will perform in a one-piece flow environment. For example, an operator might have the following sequence to produce a product in a manufacturing environment:

- unload part from machine;
- load part into machine;
- cycle start machine;
- gauge part (quality check);
- walk to assembly bench;
- assemble part;
- test part;
- pack part into container;
- walk back to first machine.

Or, in an administrative process:

- analyze insurance claim;
- check policy for eligibility;
- review adjuster's report;
- approve claim;
- enter claim into computer system;
- process payment;
- notify insured of claim status;
- file relative claim paperwork.

As stated earlier, the total amount of time required to perform this work sequence cannot exceed the stated takt time.

Once the work sequence is established and documented, it is easy to see where there are deviations to the standard work. Many times, deviating from the standard work is a signal that there is an abnormality in the process that needs to be addressed immediately. It could also indicate a quality problem when the standard work sequence is being violated.

The standard work sequence should be expected to change based on kaizen improvement activities. When this happens, the standard work documentation should be adjusted to reflect the new standard.

3 Standard Work in Process (WIP)

Standard WIP is the amount of inventory necessary to keep in the process that will allow the operator to continue operating within the work sequence. For example, in the previous standard work sequence, the part that gets loaded into the machine allows the operator the ability to walk away from the machine to perform subsequent tasks within the work sequence. Otherwise, the operator would be idle, standing in front of the machine waiting for it to finish its cycle. Standard WIP can also be used in a process such as a curing oven or electronic burn-in operation. Say a curing oven has a 20-minute cycle and the takt time is one minute. That oven would need to be loaded with 20 pieces of standard WIP. If it is a batch oven where all 20 pieces need to be cured at the same time, an additional 20 pieces would be required outside of the oven in order to allow the operator to continue in the flow process and not wait for the oven to complete its cycle.

Many refer to standard WIP as "wetting" the line, which, in the final analysis, allows the operator to continue within their work sequence, therefore optimizing productivity and output.

There are specific tools to document standard work; however, this is outside the scope of this book. Suffice it to say that standard work documentation, posted at the proper places in the workplace, is essential for its successful implementation.

Although standard work is a foundational tool in the Toyota Production System, few companies have done this well. One of the lessons we learned from studying the Toyota Production System is that a product (or document) should have a direct and unambiguous path. Standard work details this path. My sensei and mentor, Mr. Chiro Nakao from Shingijutsu, told me, "If you do not understand standard work, you do not understand the Toyota Production System" (a.k.a. Lean).

And, it's not enough just to understand it. In my early years of running operations, I had scheduled a visit from my sensei, Mr. Nakao, to perform a series of kaizen events. Upon arrival on Monday morning, Nakao declared that we need to focus on standardized work. I pushed back, stating that I already knew how to do standard work. Nakao insisted, and we went back and forth on this point. He finally asked me to accompany him to the shop floor. Nakao asked me how many operators in a particular cell were outlined on the standard work sheet which was posted at the mouth of the cell. I responded that the standard work documentation required five operators. He then asked me how many operators were actually in the cell. When I took a tally, there were eight operators in the cell! Upon discovering this, Nakao stated, "DeLuzio-san, you do not know standard work!" The Japanese mindset is that if you cannot demonstrate it, you don't know how to actually do it, regardless of how well you understand the topic from an intellectual point of view.

Investing in implementing the basic principle of standard work is worth the benefit and key to authentically implementing Lean.

KAIZEN

Kaizen is Japanese for continuous improvement.

> KAI = change
> ZEN = for the better

Based on the philosophy that what we do today should be better than yesterday and what we do tomorrow should be better than today, it means never resting or accepting status quo. A way to think of it is that kaizen is a *healthy dissatisfaction with the status quo*. Anything and everything can be improved because kaizen dictates that even though we will always strive for perfection, we will never reach a perfect state.

The key to creating a kaizen culture is to first, *briefly* celebrate your successes, not become complacent, and always be taking the next step on the never-ending journey to perfection. Is there ever a time where enough improvement is enough? My initial reaction is, "NO!" However, one must assess where to place your continuous improvement efforts relative to strategic initiatives. When I oversaw the Danaher Business System Office, I would get calls asking for assistance to 5S the mailroom in a particular division. (5S is a disciplined housekeeping and organization process which is essential for the successful implementation of all other Lean tools.) This clearly was not strategic, nor worthy of precious DBS resources. So, my first question was: how does 5S fit into our strategic initiatives? I am not suggesting that the mailroom doesn't ever need to be

5S'd; however, one needs to consider the relative benefit versus efforts of resources that can be used more strategically elsewhere.

Typical American mentality is that we all want to focus on the large, radical improvements, referred to as *kaikau* in Japanese, that seem to offer the most benefits. Beyond just being sexier, there is some merit to this breakthrough thinking and it does have a place in business (I will discuss this in more detail in Chapter 5 in the context of aligning your Lean transformation with strategy). However, I would like to remind you of the tortoise and the hare and call attention to the small, boring *kaizen* changes that occur on a daily basis. These incremental changes result in a competitive edge over the long term, and leadership must foster a culture that focuses on these smaller gains too.

There is a time and place for both kaikau and kaizen. However, Toyota won the automobile war primarily through kaizen. Strategically, the US auto manufacturers never even knew what hit them. By embracing the kaizen philosophy that's ingrained in Toyota's culture, Toyota became the number one auto manufacturer and led their global competitors in terms of market share, profitability, ROI, and quality ratings. General Motors had a unique opportunity to work with Toyota during the NUMI (New United Motors Inc.) venture in Fremont, California. Fremont was GM's worst-performing plant on a global basis. After Toyota implemented the Toyota Production System, the plant became GM's number one plant in the world. However, cultures being what they are, GM failed to radiate the lessons they learned from Toyota throughout the rest of their company. Instead, GM moved away from the kaizen philosophy and turned to large, expensive projects such as robotic automation.

Hino Motors was consistently using kaizen to reduce their truck engine development time. When Danaher's Jake Brake division was trying to become their supplier, we were implementing kaikau for breakthrough change. Hino was at 16 months by the time we had met our goal of matching their 18-month new product development cycle.

JUST IN TIME

Just in time (JIT) is a philosophy and strategy to increase efficiency and decrease waste by receiving or producing goods only as they are needed, when they are needed, in the quantity that they are needed.

I was introduced to a Midwest manufacturing company, and they claimed that they had done a great job at Lean over the past ten years. When I asked them how they incorporated takt time into their production system, they told me it does not apply to them. So, I asked how they determined what to produce. They responded that they produced product in order to maximize machine capacity, regardless of demand. For example, if they had demand for three units per hour and the equipment was capable of four units, they would produce four units so as to optimize machine utilization. This is not JIT! There are two sins here:

1. They produced excess inventory with no demand against that part.
2. They consumed precious capacity that could have been used on a part number that did, in fact, have demand placed against it.

For just in time systems to be effective, it is absolutely vital to produce with near-perfect quality or else these defects can disrupt the production process or the orderly flow and availability of product.

JIDOKA

Back in early 1900s at Toyoda Automatic Loom, the concept of jidoka was born when the first loom was stopped due to breakage of thread. Sakichi Toyoda is credited with this idea and it becoming one pillar of the Toyota Production System.

Jidoka is an automated process that is sufficiently "aware" of itself so that it will:

- Detect process malfunctions or product defects.
- Stop itself.
- Alert the operator.

Because it is difficult for workers, even when alert, to detect all defects, they wanted to transfer human intelligence to a machine. As soon as the machine detects abnormalities, it stops the manufacturing process and signals the operator. If jidoka is not utilized, a manufacturing process will continue to produce defective product until detected by an operator. This can be too late and costly.

Related to jidoka, poka yoke is a means to mistake-proof an operation and is utilized in manufacturing and administrative processes alike. An example in an administrative process is where a computer input field will ask for double input of an email address. In a manufacturing environment, a machine will not cycle unless a part is correctly fixtured.

CASE STUDY

When we were designing our production line at Jake Brake for Hino Motors in Japan, I had the opportunity to spend a day studying Hino's connecting rod machining cell. Each machine in the cell had at least one jidoka and poka yoke device. When I foolishly asked our host where they stored their defects, he responded by saying, "DeLuzio-san, we don't make defects in this cell!" This Hino cell was engineered to make near-perfect quality. We were not allowed to take pictures, but the Hino engineer offered to make a diagram of anything of interest. Trying to be polite, we only asked for two diagrams.

The very next day at our 8:00 a.m. meeting, the Hino engineer met us in the conference room. It was obvious that he had not gone home, since he was unshaven and in the same clothes as the previous day. He presented me with over a dozen drawings, stating: "DeLuzio-san, we want your production line to be like our line!" This commitment to quality had a major impact on me and my team. We successfully implemented a zero-defect line and became one of Hino's best suppliers.

THE SQDC HIERARCHY

Another basic I often default to when looking at a client's challenges (that isn't part of the foundation or pillars of Lean) is the hierarchical lens of SQDC. SQDC stands for Safety, Quality, on-time Delivery, and Cost.

For example, let's say you are debating whether or not to airship, at a high cost, a product to a customer so it arrives on time. Because on-time delivery ranks higher than cost in the SQDC model, you know it makes sense to spend the extra money to airship.

Remember from Chapter 3 that making improvements in these areas can also impact growth. I worked with a company in the UK to bring their delivery time down to 3 days from 28. This resulted in them blowing away their competition in terms of service, and their sales increased significantly as a result.

RELATE BACK TO REAL LIFE

When implementing all of these core basics and thinking through decisions that will keep your Lean transformation on track, the best advice I can give you is, "Always relate back to real life."

The chief financial officer of a diversified manufacturing company had an objective to optimize equipment efficiency. He mandated that all manufacturing facilities measure every piece of equipment for efficiency and compensated production personnel based on this metric.

This efficiency mandate led to producing millions of dollars of product that was not needed by the customer, thereby increasing the annual expense of writing off obsolete inventory. The wrong product was produced at the wrong time because plant managers were discouraging equipment die changeovers that would negatively impact their efficiency ratio. For the same reasons, they also didn't practice total preventive maintenance (TPM), which increased downtime, increased inventory levels, and deteriorated customer satisfaction scores.

When I asked this CFO why he insisted on the machine utilization metric, he responded with the fact that the company paid a lot of money for this equipment and that they needed to "get their return on investment." In turn, I asked him if he was going to drive his expensive car around the block tonight 100 times in order to get "utilization" out of it and subsequently a good "return on investment." He looked at me and said: "I never thought of it that way!" Soon after our meeting, he changed his metrics to more meaningful ones such as on-time delivery to customer request date, inventory turns, machine breakdowns, and machine changeover times.

There are other real-life analogies I like to use to show how we would never accept things in our "real," personal life that somehow are acceptable to us in the business realm. For example, when you have a backyard barbeque, do you make the hamburgers, then the hot dogs, or do you grill both at the same time? If customers want all the products you make—like they naturally would at a BBQ—your production schedule must match, as closely as possible, your customer-demand schedule. When you batch production, long changeover times cause delays in lead times, resulting in poor on-time delivery performance and excess inventories.

I had a client who had 180 days' worth of inventory and their quoted lead times to customers was seven weeks. I asked, "If you have 180 days of inventory, why are your stated lead times seven weeks? With that amount of inventory, shouldn't your lead times be only a couple of days?" The room grew silent until one executive stated, "It's because we have produced the wrong inventory!" BINGO! In their effort to avoid machine changeovers and achieve favorable absorption credit, there was no consideration given to producing product in a JIT fashion. They were making all hot dogs, then hamburgers.

In "real life," would you accept an automated grocery delivery every Saturday where you got things you didn't directly order and didn't need? In other words, product was "pushed" to you, regardless of your needs. No! In the standard practice of shopping, we choose the items we want and pull them off physical shelves.

Sometimes, we steadfastly stick to what we learned in business school when relating to real life would be more helpful. For example, in traditional cost accounting, indirect labor is viewed as waste. However, indirect labor can also be considered to be value added. In manufacturing, the operator is critical labor. They are the one directly putting the parts together. If the operator wasn't supported by team members who are supplying the parts for assembly, it would take time away from their core job.

Relating this idea back to a real-life example, think of a NASCAR driver as the operator. When they make a pit stop, what if they had to get out of the car and fill the gas, change the tires, etc.? If the goal is getting back on the track in the shortest amount of time, would it ever make sense to eliminate the pit crew as wasteful indirect labor?

To win the race in a Lean business, you've got to think of the entire supportive work sequence that must be in place to stay on track.

SUMMARY

Is your company practicing Lean or "fake Lean?" Before looking for the next magic bullet that you might read about on social media, consider doing the basics first. Remember, Toyota has been trying to perfect these basics for over 60 years. Even elementary implementation of the basics will yield significant benefits. Yet, if you strive to master these basics, a majority of your Lean initiatives will be achieved.

QUESTIONS TO ASK

- Are you consistently practicing the tenants of the Toyota Production System (just in time, jidoka, Heijunka level scheduling, standard work, and kaizen)?
- Is your organization using MRP push systems to schedule the shop floor (versus single-point scheduling)?
- Do you have an aggressive kaizen schedule for your organization?
- Are senior leaders (from all functions) actively involved, in a hands-on fashion, in kaizen events?
- Are leaders able to teach the Lean tools and principles to others?
- Are you practicing "fake Lean" by only doing the easy things, such as posters, signboards, and other cosmetics? Or, are you focusing on real process change with tools such as standard work, TPM, SMED (single minute exchange of dies), pull/flow production, etc.?
- Do you attempt to produce product in order to optimize equipment utilization rather than meet customer demand?
- Are your Lean initiatives primarily focused on cost as opposed to the hierarchy of safety, quality, delivery, and cost?
- Do you employ the same logic in making business decisions that you do to make decisions in your personal life, or do you allow performance metrics to influence decisions that are counter to Lean principles?

5

Step 3

Align Your Lean Transformation
with Strategy

During my last 18 years at the helm of a premier Lean consulting firm, I've seen time and time again how Lean teams launch into using a tool before considering how it ties into the company's overall strategy. I've also seen CEOs whose priorities lie in areas that are competing with fully investing in a Lean transformation. I recall being dumbstruck by one CEO's "strategic mindset" when he told me that his current priorities for the $7 billion industrial he led were to reduce the corporation's tax rate, implement an ERP system, and move into a new corporate office! Even though it seems obvious that results will be hit and miss without first understanding and aligning the strategic issues facing your organization, leaders don't always appreciate that they are trading off longer-term profitability for short-term gains.

The power of connecting Lean and kaizen to a strategic compass first became particularly evident to me when Danaher's Jake Brake division was in danger of going out of business in the mid to late 1980s. We were primarily serving the North American truck market, which was very reactive to domestic economic conditions, and our customer service, lead times, quality, and costs were abysmal. Kaizen was not enough; we needed a strategy and a way to deploy it by tying our Lean initiatives to our most strategic imperatives. Enter Danaher's strategy deployment process.

Under the leadership of Group Executive Art Byrne and President George Koenigsaecker, a Japanese consulting firm named Shingijutsu (meaning "New Technology") was brought in to help turn the manufacturing operation around. Little did they know at the time, but Art and

George were about to make history by starting the modern Lean movement in the United States. We rapidly began to deploy kaizen events throughout the company, organized into value streams (more on that in Chapter 6), and converted from a batch and queue "push" system to a "flow and pull" system.

After Jake Brake's initial turnaround, we introduced a basic version of the strategy deployment process. When I left Jake Brake to take the helm of the Danaher Business System, we began to roll out the strategy deployment process throughout Danaher's operating companies. Thirty years later, strategy deployment is still viewed as a critical component of the Danaher Business System.

The strategic deployment of Lean is what has differentiated Danaher's Lean approach from other Lean transformations. Danaher is often held up as the best Lean company in the US, even though the Danaher Business System is misunderstood by many. Now that GE recently appointed former Danaher CEO Larry Culp as their CEO and chairman, more business leaders may be exposed to the concept of using Lean to achieve their strategic business imperatives.

Aligning your Lean transformation with strategy is essential in keeping your efforts from flatlining over long periods of time. In this chapter, I'll examine the necessary elements:

- the strategy deployment process;
- benchmarking world class;
- identifying breakthrough.

THE STRATEGY DEPLOYMENT PROCESS

Strategy deployment (SD) is a proven methodology to convert a company's breakthrough strategy into reality by deploying key initiatives into the organization. It leverages multifunctional teams that senior management can look to for meaningful, sustainable solutions for implementing and realizing the strategy.

Let's take a closer look at what we did to turn around Jake Brake.

Due to all the manufacturing problems, Jake's customers were put on product allocation. Due to underwhelming service and quality, their largest client, Cummins Engine, which represented a third of the company's revenue, decided to produce their own version of the Jake Brake once Jake's patent expired. Overnight, this business vanished, and the remaining OEM (original equipment manufacturer) customers demanded a 33% price reduction, threatening that they would follow suit with Cummins if Jake did not buckle to their demands.

Initially, our strategy focused on radical change centered around operational performance. We developed the mantra at Danaher, "You need to earn the right to grow." If you cannot serve the customer with great quality and service, you are in no position to pursue growth objectives. We first invested in getting Jake's operations to satisfactory levels, improving quality, minimizing issues with on-time delivery, and reducing lead time to the customer.

In 1990, after we took care of the "low-hanging fruit" in the first two years of Jake's transformation, we incorporated the Hoshin Kanri process (strategy deployment) to help guide how we take Jake Brake international to counteract the cyclical nature of the business.

We targeted Mitsubishi and Hino Motors in Asia and learned that these prospective companies were developing new diesel engines in 18 months. Our new product development cycle for a new engine brake was 72 months! This was adequate for the US market, as our domestic customers weren't considered world class in this area. However, the Japanese market posed an entirely new benchmark. There were many things we needed to do in order to become competitive, but we knew that it would be impossible to enter the Japanese market without reducing our new product development cycle.

We employed a tool called value stream mapping to identify improvement opportunities. This detailed the new product development process by mapping product and information flow and calculating the respective lead time. One significant contributor to the long lead time in the current process stood out. We found that the engine lab, where we ran 500-hour tests on all new products, had a three-week changeover time from one brake model to the next. At any given point in time, there were 15 to 20 brakes waiting to be tested. To remedy this, we utilized a tool called single minute exchange of dies (SMED). The extensive engine lab changeover time was eventually reduced to one day, and there was still room for improvement.

Figure 5.1 is a visual illustration of the process we undertook to turn around Jake Brake by reaching 18 months to match Hino and Mitsubishi.

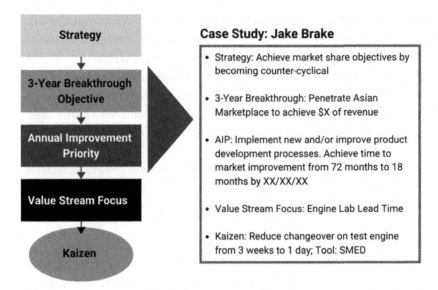

FIGURE 5.1 From Strategy Deployment to Kaizen

SMED is typically used in the manufacturing area for machinery and equipment. Had we become enamored with the SMED concept and made the tool itself the objective, it never would have found its way to the engine lab. Instead, the strategy deployment process defined the strategic objective, and we selected which tools were going to help us achieve the objective. The lesson here is that we linked our kaizen activities with strategy. I call this "kaizen with a purpose."

Jake Brake's initial success was further confirmed due to the fact that Cummins Engine eventually gave up on their version of the engine brake and brought 100% of their business back to Jake. Jake Brake became a benchmark within Danaher as well as the Lean community. After a decade, Jake's performance statistics tell the real story (see Table 5.1).

Strategy deployment creates alignment and focus for the critical piece of knowing where to apply your Lean resources. So, how do you go about pointing your efforts toward the most strategically advantageous processes and projects?

This starts at the top. I cover the role of senior leadership in Lean in Chapter 7, but senior leaders should be spending most of their time on the most strategic initiatives of the business and overseeing select, multi-functional teams to this end.

As you can see from Figure 5.2, all levels of the organization are involved in kaizen.

TABLE 5.1

Jake Brake Performance History

	Year 1	Year 10
Revenue ($ millions)	$65	$220
Headcount	550	575
Sales/Employee	$118,000	$383,000
Union	UAW	UAW
Floor Space (ft2)	240,000	240,000
Inventory Turns	2x	25x
On-Time Delivery	<20%	99%+
Productivity (Units/100 hrs)	3.0	35.0
Lead Time	85 days	2 days
Quality	75,000 PPM	<500 PPM
Development Cycle	72 months	16 months
EBIT	4%	>30%

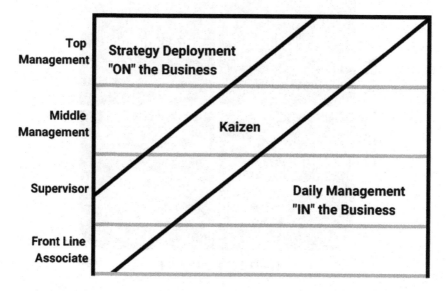

FIGURE 5.2 Daily Management

Senior leaders must determine the nature of their strategy deployment. They must ask if the strategy deployment should be focused on:

- Profitable growth?
- Operational improvements?
- Financial improvements?
- A hybrid of any of the three above?

Then, they must decide the things on which they will *not* focus. Too many times I have seen companies with 25+ strategic initiatives ... slicing their company a mile wide and a half an inch deep. Leaders must stop priding themselves on having 1,000 things to do in a day. Ultimately, nothing gets accomplished, the organization is in upheaval, and morale is at an all-time low. Use the priority filter shown in Figure 5.3 to both prioritize strategic initiatives and deselect projects.

Obviously, we are interested in those strategic initiatives that fall within the high value/high complexity quadrant. In reality, there should be little that falls into the high value/low complexity quadrant ("just do it"). Those quick-win projects don't need to be put through the strategy

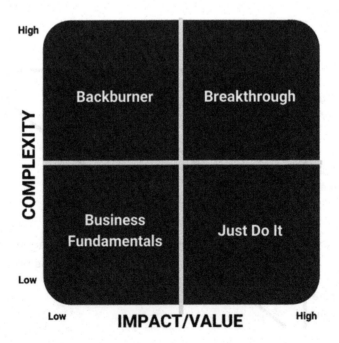

FIGURE 5.3 Strategic Priority Filter

deployment process because they can be implemented immediately with little effort. Please note that when determining the magnitude of the impact/value, this should be done in respect to the strategic plan's break-through objectives (more on that in the last section of this chapter).

The next piece is to map out the architecture of your strategy deployment initiative so that you drive to the point of impact, which is where the real value is created and the change work is manifested. This is important because if this is poorly defined, the process will fail to yield sustainable results. Exactly how to do this is complicated and beyond the scope of this book. But, in a nutshell, these are the steps:

1. Lay out the top-level matrices. There are many factors that need to be considered as to where to place top-level matrices, such as divisional or group structure, geographic structure, etc. It is also important to consider how the company is organized to recognize revenues and profits.
2. Map them all the way down to the plants so there is a line of sight through the organization that connects objectives from the top-down and bottom–up. The lowest levels of the organization are where the change actually happens. The top level has to realize they can't see everything they need to know. Multifunctional teams best define the problems, make decisions, operate, and even make mistakes.

When I was discussing strategy deployment with a CEO of a $250 million industrial company, he said, "We don't need this. I already told them what to do." This CEO clearly missed the point that his job isn't about telling others what to do, but about creating an environment where multifunctional teams are empowered to address strategic business initiatives.

In the early days of Danaher, we allowed our operating units to prepare lengthy PowerPoint presentations to "explain" why a particular goal was not achieved. We soon realized that we were practicing Plan-Do-Check-Explain rather than Plan-Do-Check-Act (see Figure 5.4). We eventually moved away from the long PowerPoint presentations and settled on only allowing the five key forms of strategy deployment in a review session. As you work through the strategy deployment process, you'll want to ensure you exercise your problem-solving muscles from the root levels of the organization. You'll do this by using the check and act components of the model to assess whether or not you are hitting your targets and course correct. You'll check your actions with quantifiable data and then act to

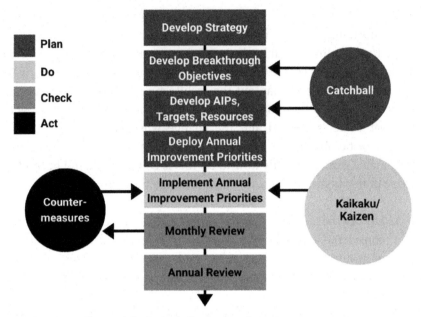

FIGURE 5.4 Seven Phases of the Strategic Deployment Process

implement any necessary countermeasures that will get you back on track.

One of the fatal flaws with strategy deployment is confusing strategic imperatives with routine daily management initiatives. We made this mistake at Danaher when we implemented strategy deployment at the divisional level. In one division, the company president listed productivity and on-time delivery as breakthrough objectives. However, this division already had well-established processes, continually high productivity, and near-perfect on-time delivery. Productivity and on-time delivery were not breakthrough items. They did face strategic issues, such as their product being engineered out by their customer base, and these are what should have been considered in their strategy deployment process.

Daily management is a way to monitor, manage, and improve the daily metrics for each function in the organization and is measured using key performance indicators (KPIs). Daily management focuses on every function, whether administrative, operational, etc. Typically, supervisors and front-line associates are heavily involved in this process and use the kaizen method to continually improve their functional daily management processes. There is no set formula for determining the KPIs for each and every function; however, a good rule of thumb is to focus your KPI metrics around the following categories:

- safety;
- quality;
- delivery;
- cost;
- growth.

Compared with strategy deployment, daily management touches almost everyone in the organization, while strategy deployment touches a select few multifunctional teams. Both methodologies use a similar tracking mechanism (the Bowling Chart in Figure 5.5) to track their progress, and both use the countermeasure problem-solving process when off track from the plan. Note that daily management is all about making continuous improvements in daily management processes rather than breakthrough improvements in a few key strategic areas. Daily management is known as working "IN" the business.

STRATEGY DEPLOYMENT BOWLING CHART

Team Name: ACME Corporation

No.	Improvement Priority	Measure	JOP 2002	2003		JAN	FEB	MAR	APR	MAY	JUN	JUL	AUG	SEP	OCT	NOV	DEC	Target
1	Prioritize and complete order entry/engineering/customer service process transition projects	Containment action to reduce order process time to 1 day std/2.5 days avg by 2/1/03	6 -16 days		Plan	6-16	1-5	1-5	1-5	1-5	1/2-5	1/2-5	1/2-5	1/2-5	1/2-5	1/2-5		1/2 - 5 days
					Actual													
2	Develop part numbers to automate order entry process	Complete by March 30, 2003	0%		Plan	25%	50%	100%	100%	100%	100%	100%	100%	100%	100%	100%	100%	100
					Actual													
3	Implement factory warehouse rebore consolidation project	Reduce rebore LT to 24-48 hrs	3 -5 days		Plan	3-5	3-5	3-5	1-2	1-2	1-2	1-2	1-2	1-2	1-2	1-2	1-2	1 -2 days
					Actual													
		Complete by 4/1/03	0%		Plan	25%	50%	75%	100%	100%	100%	100%	100%	100%	100%			100%
					Actual													
		Reduce cost $375K	$0		Plan			$31	$62	$93	$124	$155	$186	$217	$248	$279		$279
					Actual													
		Reduce inventory $250K	$0		Plan					$50	$100	$150	$200	$250				$250
					Actual													
4	Accelerate the utilization of flow process in Warren	Reduce small cptg value stream from 9.5 to 4.5 days by 5/1/03	9.5 days		Plan	9.5	7.5	6.5	5.5	4.5	4.5	4.5	4.5	4.5	4.5	4.5	4.5	4.5 days
					Actual													
		Reduce SHC & SCC cost 25% by 12/31/03	FY2002 Frozen Cost		Plan	0	10%	15%	20%	20%	20%	21%	22%	23%	24%	24%	25%	25%
					Actual													
5	Accelerate strategic sourcing initiatives	Reduce purchase price $600K	$0		Plan	$50	$100	$150	$200	$250	$300	$350	$400	$450	$500	$550	$600	$600
					Actual													
6	Eliminate black oxide process as standard	Go-No/Go by 3/1/03	No		Plan	Y/N												
					Actual													
7	Implement accurate product cost system	Achieve 95% accuracy - actual vs standard	70%		Plan	0	0%	0%	95%	95%	95%	95%	95%	95%	95%	95%	95%	95%
					Actual													

FIGURE 5.5 Strategy Deployment Bowling Chart

Robust, high-performing daily management systems are fundamental to the success of strategy deployment. If senior leadership is constantly getting dragged down to the daily management level, firefighting due to customer complaints, quality problems, etc., there will be no time for them to work "ON" the business through the strategy deployment process. Once again, a severely broken daily management process may in fact become your SD breakthrough before more strategic growth initiatives can be addressed through the SD process.

BENCHMARKING WORLD CLASS

In addition to being myopic about the view from the top, I've heard many leaders say that they are doing well because they are comparing their business with their industry competitors. Well, at five feet tall, you may be the tallest person in a pygmy village until Shaquille O'Neal walks in. I tell my clients who feel they are the best in their industry that the worst thing that can happen to them is that Toyota enters and competes in their market.

CASE STUDY

A UK company had thought they had a competitive advantage since their lead time was 28 days and competitors were at 35 days. I convinced the managing director that we could get their lead time down to three days. He initially did not believe it. We benchmarked other similar plants within Danaher where they did achieve a three-day lead time. Well, it took roughly nine months to reduce lead times to three days. The result? The company tripled revenues while increasing inventory turns from 3x to 18x and on-time delivery from 30% to 97% (to customer request date).

To get to these types of breakthrough results (more on that in the next section of this chapter), you must first benchmark against world-class standards. If you are only benchmarking within your industry, you can never be more than a mediocre company. The problem is that really good team members are often unwittingly content with mediocrity.

When a prospective diversified manufacturing client brought up Danaher in conversation, I presented a financial and operational comparison between his company, Danaher, and Fortive (a Danaher spinoff). On hearing that Danaher and Fortive's financial and operating metrics were far superior to this company, one of the senior leaders began telling me why this analysis was irrelevant and outlined all of the differences between his company and Danaher/Fortive. He went on to explain that their products were different as well as his markets, channels, customers, etc. I responded, "Yes, I agree that you are different than Danaher and Fortive. By just looking at these figures, I can clearly see how different you are!" I then went on to point out that the metrics of these two companies were, at one point, similar to his company. I asked him if he was at all interested in how they were able to significantly improve their financial and operational position from the levels that his company currently experiences. He still didn't seem interested and remained defensive.

This is a main reason that business leaders fail to appreciate the value of benchmarks, even if they are within their own industry. The inability of leaders to accurately position themselves amongst a variety of factors creates a barrier as to what can be possible. I have little hope that this company in question will make the progress they need to even approach world-class status. Actually, they are prime candidates to practice Plan-Do-Check-Explain as opposed to Plan-Do-Check-Act.

If we want to be in the upper quartile, we won't get there by just hitting the annual operating plan. We have to stretch past it.

When you task your leaders with benchmarking to world class and for long-term sustainability, they need to know what good looks like in the broader competitive universe and be willing to disrupt the status quo. As I've relayed, many leaders believe their business is different (or more complex) within their industry and need to gain the perspective that looking outside their industry can bring. Looking at different types of businesses can help you see why they are able to solve for X. If you aren't in the shipping business, you can look to FedEx for world-class standards. If you aren't in the apparel business, you can look to LL Bean for superior customer service. At Danaher, we benchmarked Disney as to how they trained their "actors." (At Disney, all associates are considered actors, even the janitor who cleans the park.)

I have been in several conversations with executives debating what exactly is world class. Is it 25 inventory turns? Six Sigma quality levels (3.4 PPM)? 15% EPS growth? I usually cut off these conversations by

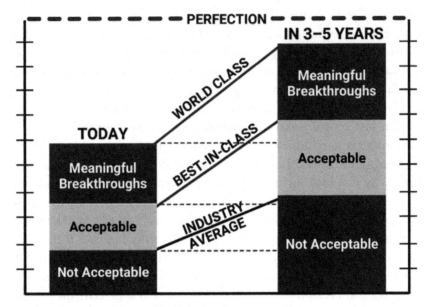

FIGURE 5.6 Benchmarking World Class Over Time

getting executives to agree that their organization is not world class. So, I like to turn the discussion to the *rate of improvement* that is required on their journey toward world class. Companies should target, at a minimum, 50% improvement annually in areas such as quality, lead time, etc. Depending on current performance, 50% may not be enough. Nevertheless, leadership should be targeting an aggressive rate of improvement to force people out of their comfort zones, which will lead to breakthrough performance.

Figure 5.6 suggests that what is a world-class benchmark today may be mediocre performance tomorrow.

There is a difference between aspiring and benchmarking to world-class standards and publicly declaring your company is now world class. Toyota doesn't say they are world class because this runs counter to kaizen philosophy.

IDENTIFYING "BREAKTHROUGH"

President Kennedy challenged us to reach the moon by the end of the decade. Fred Smith's vision of FedEx (shipping all parcels to a central point regardless of destination) was innovative, breakthrough thinking. These are two true cases of breakthrough from the respect that few believed them to be possible, let alone knew how they could be accomplished. As a matter of fact, according to an article on Entrepreneur.com, Smith's term paper at Yale only yielded a grade of C, with his professor adding, "The concept is interesting and well-formed, but in order to receive a grade better than a 'C,' the idea must be feasible."

Like Kennedy and Smith, leaders must have the courage to challenge their organization to stretch their thinking when setting breakthrough objectives. The following case study illustrates this point.

CASE STUDY: CHANGE THE LAW

I was facilitating a strategy deployment session for Danaher's Tool Group because we faced a strategic issue as it related to our largest customer, Sears. Sears Craftsman Hand Tools required that their product be produced in the USA and be labeled "Made in USA." All of Danaher's hand tools were made in the USA. However, our competitor, Stanley Works, had a distinct cost advantage because they manufactured their Craftsman tools in low-cost Asia and finished them in the USA. According to the Federal Trade Commission, Stanley Works was in compliance with the law by marking their tools "Made in USA." We did not want to move our production out of the USA as we reasoned that our Lean efforts were making us quite competitive with Stanley Works. However, we wanted to determine how to take 100% of the market share with Sears.

One executive from the Tool Group said in jest, "Let's change the law!" Everyone laughed, thinking that this was a joke. I happened to think it was breakthrough thinking! We continued to pursue the idea and through unbelievable multifunctional efforts, we succeeded in changing the Federal Trade Commission's regulation to state that "all or virtually all materials and labor must be sourced in the USA for it to be labeled 'Made in USA.'" The net result is that Stanley was forced to pull all of its manufacturing out of Asia and return it to the USA. Their costs skyrocketed, and their lead times and on-time delivery sunk to new lows. Sears became so upset with Stanley that they awarded 100% of the business to Danaher.

The "Change the Law" case study is a business example of how an idea that may seem impossible embodies the essence of a breakthrough. It is also tightly linked to strategy and customer focus.

Strategy deployment is all about creating business processes that achieve and sustain breakthrough performance. What is "breakthrough" for one organization may not be breakthrough for another. For example, an organization with poor on-time delivery may need an immediate breakthrough in this area before a growth initiative is deployed. Another organization may be better positioned to focus on growth initiatives because their on-time delivery is already at a competitive level. These are examples of what breakthrough might look like in terms of the significant benefits it provides across an organization.

Examples of breakthrough are as follows:

Financial

- Achieve upper quartile financial performance as compared with peer companies from \$X EBITA to \$Y EBITA by FY20XX.
- Achieve RONA from X% to Y% by 11/20/XX.
- Generate cash flow from 0.7% to 12% of earnings by FY20XX.

Strategic/Market Growth

- Improve revenue from systems sales from \$X to \$Y by 12/31/20XX.
- Achieve market share in motion controls from 28% to 60% by FY20XX.

Operational

- Reduce internal quality rejects from 85,000 parts per million to 2,000 parts per million by 12/31/XX.
- Improve customer satisfaction index from 60 to 98 by FY20XX.

BREAKTHROUGH EVALUATION CHECKLIST

- ☐ ties to strategy;
- ☐ is customer-focused;
- ☐ is a stretch goal;
- ☐ requires cross-functional involvement;
- ☐ results in a new system/way of doing business;
- ☐ isn't something we already know how to do.

For a breakthrough to happen, it needs to have these elements:

- Leaders are able to overcome their fears around attempting it.
- You don't know how to do it.
- It's a cross-functional team effort.

In my experience, most breakthroughs are multifunctional in nature, meaning that their achievement involves the efforts of all functions in the organization. Clearly, a big breakthrough like the first moon landing was not the job of one function or department. I served on the board of Hillenbrand, where the HR lead is an integral part of the team (along with the CEO, Lean lead, and others) that is driving them to become a world-class, diversified industrial company—because this certainly also requires talent management and development.

Since it's about enterprise-level objectives, approaching Lean transformations from only a manufacturing, operations, or engineering perspective will not achieve a breakthrough.

CASE STUDY

A fire hydrant manufacturer was trying to implement Heijunka level scheduling. On the last three days of the month, they were receiving 30% of their monthly orders. They put on overtime, worked weekends, etc. Come to find out, the sales group gave excessive discounts to their customers that accepted the product early so sales could earn their bonuses. This resulted in accelerating costs and chaos while driving down price. Instead of focusing on enterprise goals, they focused on sales goals and created a dysfunctional situation. Because this organization was focused on functional excellence rather than enterprise excellence, they weren't set up to achieve a true breakthrough.

Lastly, when a breakthrough is achieved, a standardized process should be put in place for it to become a sustainable, repeatable competitive advantage. Otherwise, the company will revert to its mediocre performance.

LESSON LEARNED

As we accomplished our new product development goal of 18 months on the Mitsubishi/Hino project, our VP of Engineering wanted to hold a party to celebrate. He only wanted to invite those employees that were involved. When I arrived, it appeared that the entire company showed up. I remarked to the VP, "I thought you were only going to invite those who were involved with Mitsubishi?" He responded, "I did!"

Right there, I knew that instead of getting to 18 months in a sustainable, repeatable manner, we had thrown other resources at the project. Since some US-based project customers had longer lead times (and quite frankly had a lot of flexibility), we borrowed their resources.

As we moved forward with Hino, we were more honest with ourselves and focused on true process innovations for all aspects of the new product development process. This also enabled us to shave two more months out of our cycle as Hino was also doing the same.

SUMMARY

It is imperative that your Lean transformation efforts support your strategic breakthrough initiatives. Over the course of time, 60–70% of your kaizen activities should be aligned with strategy deployment. Resource allocation will become a crippling issue unless you consciously decide what you are NOT going to do.

QUESTIONS TO ASK

- Do you have a robust business strategy that identifies which game you are playing and how you are going to win?
- Do you have a means to deploy your strategy within your organization?
- Are your Lean initiatives tied to your strategic imperatives?

- Does your deployment of strategy encompass the Deming Cycle of Plan-Do-Check-Act (PDCA)?
- Do you simply focus on achieving strategic goals or do you focus on those key processes within your organization which will yield the achievement of your strategic goals?
- Do you hold frequent progress reviews, with quantitative measures, of your progress toward reaching your strategic objectives?
- Are you able to divorce your daily management metrics (KPIs) from your strategy deployment initiatives (targets to improve)?
- As senior leaders, do you find that you are spending a significant portion of your time firefighting and daily management (working IN the business) versus building strategic, competitive processes (working ON the business)?
- Have you earned the right to grow your business? Are you attempting to grow despite the fact that your operational metrics (SQDC) are underperforming?
- Do you strictly benchmark against your competition or do you aspire to world-class benchmarks, even if they are outside of your industry?
- Does your organization strictly focus on achieving your annual operating plan (AOP) (budget) versus stretching beyond the AOP, reaching for breakthrough performance?

6

Step 4

Make Lean an Enterprise Endeavor

As I've said, thousands of companies are "doing Lean" for different reasons, perhaps to save costs, to create more value for the customer, or to optimize a single function in the organization. Maybe it's because the sales department had to hit a target. Recall the earlier example of the fire hydrant manufacturer whose sales department was meeting quotas by pushing through 30% of their orders in the last three days of every month. Their severe discounts to incentivize customers to take product they didn't need disrupted manufacturing operations, added overtime expenses, and squeezed margins at both ends. Clearly, the company was not adopting Lean as an enterprise endeavor because only the sales team was winning.

If you think about your personal overall health, it may do you some good to go on a 30-day diet to lose ten pounds. You will feel improved after losing the weight, but we know that diets are not a long-term wellness strategy. To truly become healthier, we need to learn to consume food differently on an everyday basis. Plus, we need to do other things consistently, like go for check-ups, get at least seven hours of sleep, use our brains, and exercise. We know we need to take a whole-body approach.

Most companies approach their Lean transformation from a functional perspective and insist on running their overall organization in the same traditional way that they did in the 1970s. The Lean organization needs to challenge their organizational reporting structure, compensation system, management accounting system, and overall metrics—which are most likely driving dysfunctional behaviors.

For example, compensation awards are centered around lagging metrics, such as profit, return on investment, and working capital turns, rather than leading, sustaining indicators that are actually reflective of overall operational, commercial, and financial success. Remember that COPQ (cost of poor quality) is a good leading indicator (to profitability and customer satisfaction) because it represents anywhere from 15–25% of revenues. Lean organizations need to evolve their focus to be on the drivers of success.

To optimize everything in an organization in a way that the benefits keep coming for the entire Lean Trilogy that we discussed in Chapter 3, we'll focus on the following in this chapter:

- enterprise kaizen versus point kaizen;
- value stream management;
- mura, muri, and muda;
- Lean accounting.

ENTERPRISE KAIZEN VS. POINT KAIZEN

I've worked with numerous organizations over the past 18 years who started their Lean transformations with point kaizens but never graduated to enterprise kaizens. Sustainable results that combat flatlining can only be achieved via an enterprise focus that *has hands-on involvement from senior leadership*.

Some do view Lean on the front-line, operational level—that is far removed from senior leadership—and treat it like a series of box-ticking. This appears like, "We hung that poster, we moved those machines, we drew yellow lines on the floor, and we improved productivity by 8%, so we're making progress with Lean." This would be through single-point scheduling executing a series of point kaizens. Point kaizens are usually focused on a single operation or process, and when compared with enterprise kaizen, easier to accomplish. Don't get me wrong: point kaizens are necessary in a Lean transformation. However, more is required. In addition to processes and functions, the entire organization must be transformed in order to truly become a Lean organization.

Enterprise transformation is usually more difficult for the following reasons:

- It requires an extremely high degree of Lean IQ from its senior leaders.
- Its leaders must be working as one.
- All functions in an organization must also have a firm grasp on this Lean IQ, in addition to fully adopting and internalizing the Lean transformation plan.
- All functions must be willing to conduct business in the Lean way, breaking away from traditional management practices.
- Functional leaders must be able to cooperate with one another and work for the common goal of the enterprise rather than the optimization of their particular function.
- It requires a different metric and compensation program, which should be designed to reward behaviors consistent with Lean practices and philosophy.
- It requires Lean accounting (more later in this chapter).

In the Lean Enterprise Institute blog (www.lean.org/LeanPost/Posting.cfm?LeanPostId=1011, February 25, 2019), friend and colleague Orry Fiume, former VP of Finance of Wiremold, talked about the leadership of CEO Art Byrne and his senior team:

> But, as Art understood from his days at Danaher, you can't make the transition to Lean unless the management team acts as one. Our new structure of the 12 teams reporting to the senior management team (as a single entity) reinforced this. We couldn't afford to have our associates getting different answers depending on which vice president they asked. We also couldn't afford to have any one function going in its own direction. Our customers just saw us as one entity, The Wiremold Company. Any behavior that didn't conform to this was just waste.

CASE STUDY

In working with a diversified manufacturing company that has been on a Lean journey for over ten years, I found they were still using MRP (a "push" system) to schedule their various manufacturing departments rather than a "single-point" scheduling system which supports the Lean concepts of "pull" production and Heijunka level loading. In order for single-point scheduling to be successful, a sales and operations planning (S&OP) process is required.

To accomplish a Lean S&OP process, all facets of the organization need to work together and be on the same page. Sales, marketing, engineering, finance, manufacturing, production planning, supply chain, and human resources all need to be active participants in the unified goal of serving the customer in the most efficient and profitable way. Unfortunately, functional objectives were a major barrier to these groups working together. This organization was somewhat successful at point kaizens but fell short when it came to improving the overall enterprise.

In reality, it makes sense that for Lean to achieve lasting results for the entire enterprise, it must stem from enterprise-wide kaizens that come from the top of the organization. An enterprise kaizen is aimed at changing systematic, traditional behaviors across all functions. For example, in the fire hydrant company story at the beginning of this chapter, that type of dysfunction wouldn't happen if sales compensation were also tied to on-time delivery and forecast accuracy in addition to orders. The S&OP process must be an enterprise-wide endeavor because it does affect every part of the company.

As illustrated in Figure 6.1, enterprise kaizens require the efforts of senior management, middle management, the front lines, and everyone

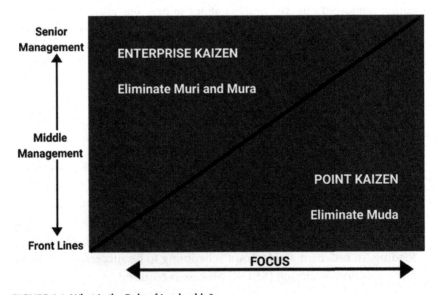

FIGURE 6.1 What Is the Role of Leadership?

in between. It's about optimizing value streams from the top–down, rather than just optimizing individual functions.

VALUE STREAM MANAGEMENT

Getting away from running the enterprise in the traditional functional manner requires thinking and restructuring in terms of value streams. Value streams support transformation because they serve as a "company within a company." What does that mean? It means that the value stream has full profit and loss responsibility, is multifunctional in nature, and contains all of the necessary resources to be successful. A value stream is typically organized around a product family; however, it can be organized around common processes. I have seen value streams where the order-taking and customer service function was imbedded into the operation. Some value streams contain their own finance, maintenance, and tooling personnel. Yes, some of these resources need to be shared amongst value streams; however, an attempt should be made to allow the value stream to be as standalone as possible in order to directly service their customer base.

What exactly is a value stream? We define value stream in our Lean Horizons training suite as:

> A grouping of all of the processes necessary to bring a product or service from its raw state to a finished product or service that is profitably saleable to a customer.

An example of a manufacturing value stream is depicted in Figure 6.2. An administrative value stream is depicted in Figure 6.3.

When you just have VPs of functional areas in a traditional matrix organization, the customers are the last to be considered, and the people who report into that function mainly have an allegiance to that functional VP. For example, those underneath the VP of Sales are focused on optimizing sales. But, if you have a VP of a value stream that is focused on serving a particular customer, everyone underneath that VP is also focused on serving that customer. This is analogous to wanting to improve your golf game and only frequenting the driving range. Since the driver is only used in about 10% of the game, you should be investing

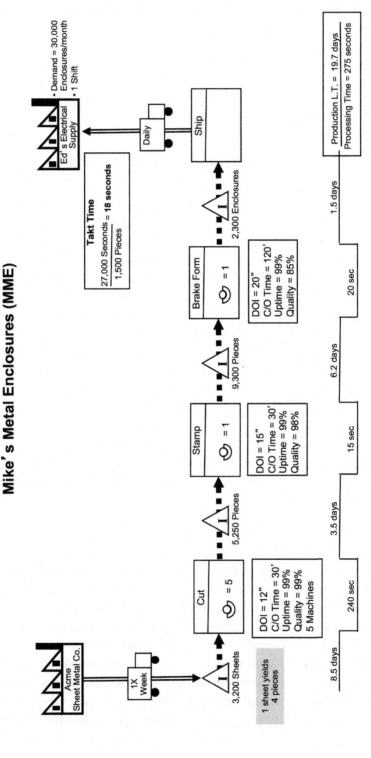

FIGURE 6.2 Manufacturing Value Stream Example

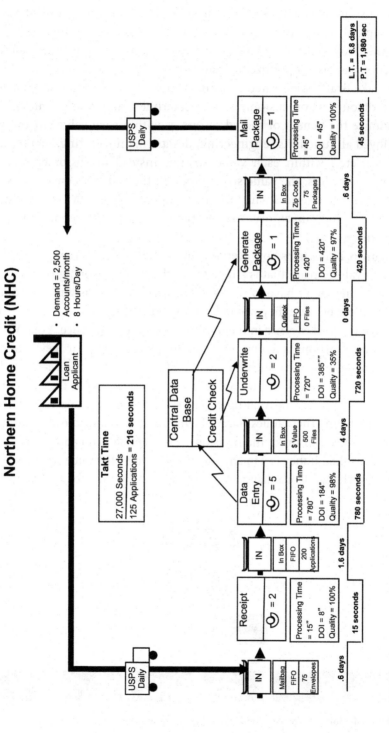

FIGURE 6.3 Administrative Value Stream Example

90% of your practice time across all the other areas, from course strategy to chipping and putting. Just like you have to put all of these areas together well to be really good at the game, you have to integrate all the functional areas to optimize the value for the customer.

At Jake Brake, we created and ran customer-centric value streams for each of our major customers like Caterpillar and Mack Trucks. To maximize the benefit of shared resources within each value stream, we deployed all functions (engineering, design, manufacturing, marketing, finance, etc.) within each value stream. Instead of customer service taking the orders, the value stream took in the orders to encompass all the things that need to happen in the process, such as order entry, manufacturing, inventory management, logistics, warehousing, and accounting.

Figure 6.4 illustrates how everyone in the value chain is reporting into a VP of a value stream that is aligned with the customer or a group of customers. They don't have to worry about whether to satisfy the customer or their boss because they would be doing both by default.

While this makes sense in theory, it's hard to do in practice. Your VP of whatever function is going to have to give away their keys to the kingdom—the one to which they spent years trying to advance—in order to now become the VP of the value stream. In many cases, the functional VP may not possess the multifunctional skills necessary to successfully lead a value stream. Therein lies the problem. These functional leaders are the ones who need to make the decision to manage the company in a value stream fashion. If they feel in any way threatened by the value stream structure, the change won't happen. This is where the CEO of the company

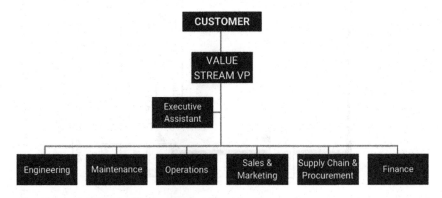

FIGURE 6.4 **Multifunctional Organization Aligned to Customer**

comes into play. They must have the understanding and maturity to make the hard calls necessary to move to a value stream approach. I'll cover more on how the leadership culture needs to change in order to prevent flatlining on Lean in the next chapter, but it's important to consider the Lean Trilogy in establishing the non-zero-sum organizational structure and stop self-defeating behavior relative to the enterprise.

MURA, MURI, AND MUDA

I've established why enterprise transformations and the structure that supports them lead to long-term results with Lean. Notice in Figure 6.1 how enterprise kaizens are oriented toward eliminating muri and mura at all levels of the organization. Both are higher-level types of waste. Muri means unreasonableness and mura means unevenness. Both of these forms of waste are typically generated by the traditional and flawed policies that are set by leadership.

The problem is that most Lean efforts are instead focused on muda (Japanese for waste), which has to do with eliminating different types of operational waste at the organization's lower levels. The Toyota Production System describes seven types of muda:

1. waste from motion;
2. waste from inventory;
3. waste from overproduction;
4. waste from defects;
5. waste from transportation;
6. waste from walking;
7. waste from over-processing.

Typically, the reduction of the seven wastes comes from point kaizens and line associates who have hands-on experience with the operations to be able to identify that which is non-value-added. For example, a California-based manufacturer was set up in a traditional batch-and-queue process. There was considerable waste, and the operators seemed to do an excessive amount of walking. As we know, walking is non-value-added. We calculated that one particular operator, Kay, walked approximately six miles per day, which is equivalent to walking from

San Jose to St. Louis on an annual basis. When the shop was reconfigured to a cellular manufacturing approach, Kay's walk time was virtually eliminated.

On the other hand, efforts toward eliminating mura and muri are typically generated by the organization's leaders, and they are often caused by management in the first place. The front-line associate has little opportunity to eliminate these two forms of waste.

While leaders must understand all forms of waste so they can actively take a role in eliminating waste, they must be attuned to the fact that they are often the direct cause of mura and muri. Unevenness often can be eliminated by managers through level scheduling and careful attention to the pace of work.

MURA CASE STUDY

A client of mine was desperately trying to create a Lean organization, but they had a sales pricing strategy that encouraged steep discounts at the end of each fiscal quarter. The objective was to book more sales in that quarter ... a form of window dressing to the financial statements. Their management failed to realize that they were taking sales volume from the next quarter, which usually manifested itself in very low shipping volume in the first three or four weeks of the new quarter. Because of this sales policy, customers were trained as to when to order product to take advantage of pricing discounts, regardless of their true demand for that product.

The net result was a "hockey stick" effect, where 70% of the volume was shipped out during the last two weeks of the quarter. This "unevenness" placed tremendous pressure on the manufacturing and distribution associates. In fact, there were times when the manufacturing operation would stop producing at the end of the quarter, and manufacturing personnel were sent to the distribution warehouse to ship product.

You can see that their plans to level-load production were totally undermined by this mura practice created by the sales management team. Only leadership has the power to set the culture of a Lean organization and to right this wrong. If this sales leadership were organized under a value stream, this policy would never have flown.

Muri often means that equipment and operators are overburdened. They are running at a higher pace or for longer periods of time than the equipment is designed to handle or which is allowed in appropriate workforce management.

ELIMINATE MURI AND MUDA CASE STUDY

When we conducted a value stream mapping exercise for the claims process of a large property and casualty company, we found more than a dozen management signoffs and approvals for each claim in the process. These signoffs contributed to the massive lead time to process a claim and many of them were redundant or weren't necessary because 99% of all claims were approved. For example, a claims adjuster had approval authority up to $5 million. If the claim in question were one dollar over the $5 million approval authority, the claim would have to be submitted for management approval.

By eliminating many of the signoff points, as well as making other improvements, we were able to reduce the lead time to process a claim by 70%.

Once again, this muri and muda was created by senior leadership. Even though they could see its ill effects, the local management and front-line associates had little recourse with this mandate.

I can vividly recall the time I witnessed a Japanese sensei give the best explanation of why a senior leader must internalize the concept of waste. Our sensei had asked a senior leader, "Why is there so much inventory on the shop floor?" As he started giving excuses, the sensei asked for the leader's wallet and placed it upon a pile of inventory nearby. Then, he signaled the group to move on with the tour. Being uncomfortable, the leader asked about his wallet and why it was being left behind. The sensei asked the leader why he is concerned, and the leader replied, "I'm concerned because I have money in my wallet." The sensei paused and said, "Don't you understand that inventory is also money? You are quite comfortable leaving the company's money on the shop floor in the form of inventory, but you are not comfortable leaving your own money behind?" The leader got the message.

LEAN ACCOUNTING

As we've been reviewing, companies need to get away from ingrained dysfunctional behaviors across the board in order to achieve lasting transformations. The traditional accounting systems we were taught in college run counter to Lean philosophy and will kill a transformation when used. Full disclosure: I'm an accountant by trade and pioneered the concept of Lean accounting in the United States in my role as CFO at Danaher's Jake Brake division.

There is a difference between Lean accounting and accounting for Lean. Lean accounting suggests that Lean principles are applied to the accounting process in order to remove waste from the process itself. Accounting for Lean refers to providing financial information to leaders in order to make decisions that are in concert with the principles of Lean. Accountants can be Lean's worst enemy. I once met a controller who wanted to financially justify every Lean kaizen event. As a former CFO, I am not able to provide financial justification to some aspects of Lean. For example, performing a 5S kaizen is difficult to quantify, but we all know it is the right thing to do. Don't let your financial people derail your Lean initiatives.

We have to be willing to throw out old measures and evaluate capital with a Lean eye. When value streams are set up, you also need to practice value stream accounting and forget things like absorption accounting, purchase price variance, and traditional capital justification because they promote the wrong behaviors. They may make the accounting function look great, but don't do any justice to the enterprise as a whole.

For example, let's take a look at absorption variances. If I have a plant that has $1 million of fixed overhead and produces 1 million units a year, the cost of fixed overhead is $1 per unit. If I make 500,000, the cost is $2 per unit. So, I need to make more if I want to reduce my cost per unit. But are costs really reduced? No, I just deferred my costs into the balance sheet in the form of inventory. Eventually these costs need to come out as inventory in the form of cost of goods sold or be written off as obsolete inventory. Absorption costing runs counter to the Lean concept of just in time—making the right product at the right time—and promotes creating excess inventory without demand. In the short term, absorption accounting shows fake profits by transferring costs to the balance sheet. In reality, we are just deferring the problem and will need to recognize these capitalized costs sooner or later.

CASE STUDY

One of my clients had poor on-time delivery with significant past-due orders. I asked about a large amount of finished goods inventory in their warehouse, and they replied that they built this inventory ahead of when the customer needed it, but that it's not a problem since the customer has already paid for it and it was not on their books. I asked the general manager if he considered that by producing this inventory that was not needed by the customer, he violated the principles of just in time. He defended his position by claiming that he was able to generate revenue early.

Being a past accountant, I explained to him that based on his shipping terms, he technically cannot recognize this revenue until the customer took possession of the goods. But the real point is that he consumed (stole) resources that were needed for his other orders that were past due. This is a clear example of the accounting system driving un-Lean behaviors.

Perhaps your purchasing leader wants to look like a hero by over-buying large quantities of inventory to get a volume discount and artificially creating a favorable purchase price variance (PPV)? While this seems like a good idea on the surface, it runs counter to the Lean concept of just in time and, most likely, this bargain inventory will need to be written off as obsolete inventory.

Let's apply Lean accounting to overhead costs. Variable overhead concerns things that fluctuate with volume, such as electricity, oil, supplies, and tooling (due to wear). Fixed overhead is set costs like salary. In a traditional cost accounting system, these overhead costs are placed in one overhead pool and are allocated to products based on some arbitrary allocation method such as labor or machine hours. In contrast, Lean accounting attempts to *directly* assign these costs to a product and/or value stream, thereby reducing the need for arbitrary overhead allocations. The result? Better accountability and more accurate product costs.

CASE STUDY

At Jake Brake, we assigned most overhead costs to each value stream rather than arbitrarily allocating these costs. One of these costs was machine depreciation. Upon reviewing his actual cost (note that in a Lean environment, the use of standard costing is discouraged) for his product, the value stream leader did not understand his machine depreciation charge of $75 per unit. When I explained the concept of depreciation, he asked, "If I were to reduce the number of machines in my manufacturing cell, would this charge be reduced?" He indicated that he had eight CNC machines and he only needed six. I told him that his depreciation charge would go down by approximately $25 per unit. He promptly removed the machines from his value stream and received the cost benefit.

About one month later, I received a capital appropriation request (CAR) for two new CNC machines totaling $500,000. I promptly tore the CAR up, threw it in the trash, and directed the requestor to go to the excess equipment area and pick up his two machines.

In a traditional accounting environment, we would never uncover the fact that the value stream contained excess equipment. The Lean accounting system saved the company $500,000 in capital via the direct charging of overhead costs to the value stream.

I was the first in the country to do this type of analysis and became known as the "Father of Lean Accounting." It was born from simply doing what I thought was the right thing to do in respect to Lean principles.

SUMMARY

Companies that don't focus on the enterprise as a whole will never realize the true potential that Lean has to offer and will continue to flatline in their results. Extend beyond functional point kaizens and recognize and address how your organizational structures and policies may be driving enterprise waste in the forms of mura and muri.

QUESTIONS TO ASK

- Are your Lean initiatives strictly focused on functional "point kaizens" versus multifunctional "enterprise kaizens"?
- Do you primarily view Lean as an operational/manufacturing tool? Or do you view it as an enterprise approach which applies to all functions within your organization?
- Do all functional leaders have a firm understanding of Lean principles and practices?
- Is your organization structured into multifunctional value streams or do you attempt to employ a traditional functional structure?
- Do your value streams clearly depict a future state vision for your organization?
- Have you considered the mura and muri your organization's policies, practices, and procedures have created?
- Is your sales team responsible for inventory levels, on-time delivery, and lead time?
- Does your manufacturing group have clear visibility toward true customer demand?
- Do you have a robust sales & operations planning process that informs the operation of true customer demand? Or, are your forecasts primarily financially driven and of little help to the organization?
- Are your compensation and incentive systems enticing dysfunctional behaviors (counter to Lean principles)?
- Do you still employ traditional management accounting systems that promote dysfunctional behaviors, such as the building and purchasing of unnecessary inventory?
- Do you have an accurate assessment of your true product costs and gross margins?

7

Step 5

Use Lean Principles to Evolve Your Company's Culture

If Lean is an enterprise endeavor, culture is the glue that holds the entire infrastructure together. To be clear, I'm not just talking about a "Lean culture," I'm asking you to use Lean principles as you think about evolving the culture of the entire company. A company's culture is the reflection of the sum total of the various beliefs, values, and behaviors demonstrated by its employees.

On one of my many visits to Toyota in Japan, I asked a senior Toyota executive how they could allow their competition into their factories for benchmarking purposes. The executive responded: "What they need to know they cannot see." What he was referring to was Toyota's culture and how employees think and behave at Toyota. The culture is the "secret sauce." It's what can attract top talent and motivate them to keep improving. According to Professor James L. Heskett, author of *The Culture Cycle* (Pearson FT Press, 2011), "it can account for 20–30% of the differential in corporate performance when compared with 'culturally unremarkable' competitors." Giving mindshare to culture is important, but it isn't easy.

Former Danaher CEO Larry Culp (now Chairman and CEO of General Electric) said that the "Danaher Business System is our culture." Danaher so ingrained the Lean philosophy in all aspects of the enterprise that DBS actually defined Danaher's culture. More than a set of tools, it became a way of thinking, a way of life.

I like to say, "The hard stuff is easy and the soft stuff is hard." The "easy, hard stuff" is mastering all the technical aspects of Lean: standard work, takt time, flow and pull production, and quality improvements. The "hard, soft stuff" is all about people and managing change, which means how you indoctrinate the workforce into using those tools. It's about aligning behaviors with your organization's core values so you can see those values in action. I was conducting an evaluation at a company who said one of their core values was "respect for people." The leader who invited me set up the meeting on a weekend starting at 10:00 a.m. on a Saturday and carrying over to two hours on a Sunday morning. If he's dragging his team in on a weekend, why not go a little longer on Saturday to prevent people from having to work on Sunday? He wasn't "walking the talk" because there clearly was no respect for his team's personal time.

I have seen many companies claim they are customer-focused; however, they insist on measuring their on-time delivery to customer *promise* date as opposed to customer *request* date. Not only does this fail to recognize the needs and requirements of the customer, it also sends a message about the ultimate culture of the organization to its customers and associates. If one of an organization's core values is to be customer-focused, leaders would embrace what that means, break out of their functional organization structure and reorganize into customer-focused value streams.

Keep in mind that values and principles without underlying processes are merely slogans. I like that so much that I've made it my personal tagline. These are some of the principles that I've adopted and strive to implement with everything I do:

- respect for people;
- FLOW first, PULL where you can't, never, ever PUSH;
- solve problems at the "lowest possible, highest necessary" level in the organization;
- no opinions unless you go to gemba (must observe problem);
- assure quality before passing on a product or service;
- don't let perfect get in the way of better;
- use your brain before you use your wallet;
- it's not a process unless it's documented;
- in God we trust, all others bring data;
- the principles of just in time;
- *healthy* dissatisfaction with the status quo;
- blameless environment.

Similarly, when you are creating lasting transformation, it's important to cultivate a change management culture. To do this, employees need to know what's in it for them. Do they benefit from the change in addition to the shareholders? When they succeed in making processes more efficient, will it enrich their work lives, grow the business, and provide security for all, or will it eliminate jobs?

More than incentives, plans, and resources, managing complex change requires vision, and that comes from the top. In this chapter, we'll cover how senior leaders set the tone for evolving the culture in these four areas:

- define leadership's role;
- deal with naysayers (the Toyota Change Model);
- develop a healthy dissatisfaction with the status quo;
- delegate problem-solving.

DEFINE LEADERSHIP'S ROLE

I was talking with the CEO of a multibillion-dollar company. He was blaming their flatlined results on everyone else. This reminds me of an ancient Chinese proverb, "The fish rots from the head."

The power of Lean rippling through your organization and taking off over the long haul requires the CEO to be the champion of it. This happens by centering it around cultural *evolution* rather than cultural *change*. I learned a long time ago that I'd get thrown out of a company if I came in suggesting that the culture had to change. The truth is that there are always good aspects to established cultures that one can harness and grow. The danger is when companies believe they walk on water because they have an iconic brand or a storied history. In truth, there are very often gaps between how a company perceives itself and how they are really performing. The CEO needs to bring these areas to light and define a vision that can serve as the architectural drawing for building the desired culture.

To avoid having an understaffed, ineffective Lean organization, the CEO must also take a hard look at their beliefs, actions, and expectations around Lean. As CEO, these are the questions you must ask yourself:

- Have I delegated the responsibility for my Lean transformation, or do I believe it rests on my shoulders?

- Do I understand how to customize a Lean organization to meet our strategic objectives?
- Do I believe in the power of Lean to meet our strategic objectives to the extent that I'm willing to invest in the appropriate Lean resources?
- Am I so preoccupied with other priorities that I'm not seeing that Lean could be the solution to many, if not most, of our problems?
- Am I already so content with my business results that I don't feel the need to customize a Lean organization to achieve results?
- Due to the lack of Lean success in my industry, do I have little faith that my investment in Lean will have any tangible benefits?
- Did I select a Lean leader to simply act as a figurehead for the purposes of window dressing in the annual report?

The CEO must carefully consider the structure of their organization and properly staff it for a Lean transformation. First, to challenge the status quo by indoctrinating Lean principles into the culture, the head of Lean must directly report to the CEO. This ensures the CEO will carve out time to be involved. Instead of having the head of Lean be strictly technical, the CEO should select someone who is strategic and understands all the functions of the enterprise. They must look for a leader who can model best practices by being hands-on, which helps foster a culture where everyone is engaged and empowered. Understand, however, that the ultimate responsibility for driving change and results in the organization rests with the CEO, not the head of Lean.

I recently visited with the Vice President of Lean for an $8 billion diversified manufacturer of consumer products who was interested in my experience with the creation of the Danaher Business System. They had begun their transformation three years earlier, and I asked him how his Lean organization was structured at the corporate office as well as within his businesses. He responded, "You are looking at it!" He went on to say that their various businesses throughout the world had no Lean resources whatsoever. The good news was that this Lean VP reported to the CEO. The bad news was that he was the only person assigned to a Lean role within his organization. I politely told him that he is not set up to succeed, and that we need to address his organizational situation immediately.

It's critical to have Lean leaders in each business unit because they act as culture carriers. Think of it this way: Jesus had 12 disciples to help him spread the Word. Imagine if he had gone it alone instead? Your head of

Lean cannot go it alone either. Just like a shepherd leans on his "staff" for physical support, staff positions serve as support to the line positions who are charged with delivering results and creating a Lean culture. These additional Lean resources are not responsible for Lean success, but for spreading the word and achieving their objectives. The primary role of all Lean resources, however, is to teach others how to fish. They must always be acting as Lean coaches, whether they reside in your corporate office or within your various businesses. I'm sure you know the Lao Tzu proverb, "If you give a man a fish, you feed him for a day; if you teach a man to fish, you feed him for a lifetime."

While leading the DBS office at Danaher, every time we got a request for Lean resources, I asked, "Who will be the target for us to transfer knowledge and know-how?" Many times, they would respond that they simply needed a project completed and viewed the DBS office as just another set of resources. I refused to send assistance if I was not convinced that we would be able to "teach others how to fish."

At Danaher, we also used the DBS office to train future leaders in our DBS methodology. Presidents and vice presidents, as well as other leaders, came out of their respective roles and worked full-time in the DBS office, anywhere from 6 to 12 months. When they returned to their line or staff role, they led DBS in their line role of their organization with almost a religious fervor. Ultimate career success at Danaher was contingent upon one's ability to lead and achieve results utilizing the Danaher Business System. The DBS Lean office played a major role in the evolution of Danaher's culture.

There are many ways to staff a Lean organization which are beyond the scope of this book. The design of such an organization should complement the organization's culture and be customized. For example, should there be a centralized approach? A decentralized approach? A hybrid? Like with your head of Lean, careful consideration should be made as to the qualifications of your various Lean resources. You will need strategic thinkers, leadership coaches, technicians who are well versed in the various Lean tools, etc. Not all Lean resources are equal and that's okay— you don't want them to be. You will need a diverse set of talents to accomplish your Lean transformation. You'll find some criteria for evaluating your Lean consultants in this book's addendum, and much of this can be applied to bringing Lean resources on staff as well.

When everyone in the organization understands that the CEO really believes in and knows Lean because the CEO is actually doing it and not just watching from the sidelines, a shift happens. The CEO's enthusiasm for the process and hard work of Lean to yield long-term results (not just short-term gains) is contagious.

Toyota Chairman Fujio Cho describes the three keys to Lean leadership as:

1. Go see.
2. Ask why.
3. Show respect.

1 Go See

"Go see" means senior management is spending time at the gemba, Japanese for where the work gets done. It's about directly experiencing and assessing. How can you attempt to solve a problem without seeing it first? We have learned from our friends at Toyota that a leader is not allowed to opine on a problem if they have not observed the situation firsthand.

Leaders should regularly participate in daily management gemba walks on both the factory floor as well as the office. Regular participation as a full-time member of kaizen teams is the only real way for leaders to learn the essence of Lean. I have heard that you cannot learn the game of golf by watching videos or by reading books alone. You must swing the club and go to the golf course (gemba) and practice regularly to improve your game (kaizen). Lean is no different, with hands-on experience being the only way to truly learn.

2 Ask Why

"Ask why" means senior management is asking the right questions on a daily basis. I recently went into a company that had 180 days of inventory and a 7-week lead time, and they weren't shipping to a customer. I asked, "With a six-month supply of inventory, why are your lead times seven weeks? Why can't you just ship it immediately?" I knew the answer, but I wanted them to realize that they actually had the wrong inventory on hand. This type of questioning allows others to come to a realization that they otherwise would not consider. The leader does not need to know all of the answers; they must know how to ask the right questions. "Why?" is perhaps the most powerful question one can ask when trying to solve a problem.

3 Show Respect

"Show respect" and the "respect for people" principles have been given a lot of hype in the Lean press. Yet, I witness this principle being violated on a regular basis. Most times, lack of respect for the individual is not a blatant, obvious behavior on the part of leaders. It manifests itself in a number of ways that are hidden and is usually a result of omission rather than commission. For example, expecting employees to solve problems without giving them the time and tools is a lack of respect for the employee. Allowing employees to have to operate wasteful processes without any means of improving them is another form of disrespectful leadership. Leaders need to remove barriers to change, provide the resources, and model the behavior they expect from those reporting to them. Any deviation from this is a direct lack of respect.

Using Lean as a headcount-reduction tool is perhaps the ultimate sign of disrespect for the employee. When employees are asked for their improvement ideas, they can't feel like they'll put themselves or their colleagues out of a job when they give honest input. Cultivating trust between management and labor is essential for a positive and lasting Lean transformation, whether the organization is unionized or not.

Leaders should be prepared to address the workforce when they are asked the question: "What happens to my job when it is eliminated as a result of Lean activities?" I assisted one client with developing the following policy:

- The tenants of our Lean transformation will encourage and value:
  - the development of a multi-skilled workforce;
  - flexibility and willingness to change;
  - a continuous improvement mindset;
  - cross-functional teamwork.
- When the elimination of non-value-added activities creates excess resources, we will make every attempt to redeploy identified excess resources through:
  - growth in business;
  - natural attrition;
  - less reliance on temporary and/or seasonal staff;
  - deployment to full-time improvement teams;
  - in-sourcing opportunities where strategically feasible;
  - retraining for redeployment into other areas of the business.

Table 7.1

Examples of Non-Negotiables

NON-NEGOTIABLE	LEADERSHIP	MANUFACTURING	ADMIN
Flow first, pull where you can't, NEVER push		●	●
Use standard work for all processes		●	●
Decide what you are NOT going to do and adjust metrics accordingly	●	●	●
Use takt time on all capital, inventory, and manning decisions		●	●
Don't give opinions unless you've observed the problem first-hand	●	●	●
Use your brain before your wallet (creativity before capital)	●	●	●
Standardize the problem-solving process and insist on its use	●	●	●
Flow cells counterclockwise and don't have chairs in them		●	
Insist on visual management	●	●	●
All leaders learn to teach Lean and run a kaizen event	●		
Have a respect for people and blameless environment	●	●	●
Leaders participate in one kaizen event per quarter	●	●	●
Offer and utilize continuous education on Lean (books, kaizen events, seminars, consultants)	●		●

Note that this company did not guarantee employment. In reality, this is not feasible, and a company must allow for adjustments in headcount to counteract a poor economy or business condition. The key is not to commit the cultural sin of linking headcount reductions to a *Lean transformation* in any way. Remember, we are asking employees to participate in a hands-on manner to improve the various processes of the business. If employees see this as a path to unemployment, there will be little if any contribution from them in improving the business. It is important for leadership to carefully craft this message and assure that all leaders in the organization are consistent in their communications with employees.

A leader must set what I call "non-negotiables." These are the set of requirements that will not be compromised in a Lean transformation. Table 7.1 has examples of non-negotiables.

In 1995, then President and CEO of Danaher, George Sherman, said, "The Danaher Business System (DBS) is NOT optional." That's the type of mandate that can only come from the top. It reinforces that DBS is essential because Danaher is an operating company, not a holding company. On January 25, 2016, Matt Trerotola, Colfax's CEO, said, "If we are not growing, the Colfax Business System (CBS) is not working." This sent the message that Matt smartly views his Lean transformation as a growth exercise for the business and the employees, not a simple cost-cutting exercise. In this statement, he was reinforcing a growth culture.

Although it may sound like it from these examples, establishing non-negotiables isn't something that is dogmatic. The "do it my way" model of leadership is long outdated, and we learned in the 1970s that the "do it your way" empowerment style isn't necessarily effective. The Lean leader leads by kaikaku and kaizen. Again, kaikaku means radical change and kaizen has to do with continuous incremental changes. To achieve both of these, they need to connect back to the vision and create a narrative and personal way of being that inspires action.

Kan Higashi and Gary Convis, senior leaders at NUUMI, said, "Lead the organization as if you have no power." When so many are hell bent on deploying a metric (such as improve quality by 50%), this statement is perfect for helping us to remember what the leader's mindset should be. Lean leaders must be willing to:

- think through the people side (a.k.a., the hard stuff), actively engaging in developing people and helping the team function better;
- break away from the traditional organizational/functional models;

- set aside egos and put the team solution ahead of their individual interests;
- focus on sustainable processes that yield results rather than the result itself;
- cultivate a blameless environment that shifts the focus from the employee to the process.

DEAL WITH NAYSAYERS

Although I am a firm believer that you must focus on the process as opposed to the individual, the fact remains that there will be people who do not share your vision, who are set in their ways, and simply do not want to change. I refer to these people as naysayers.

When you are making meaningful changes, you want people who are energizing it rather than fighting it. Figure 7.1 depicts the Toyota Change Model. In my experience, naysayers can make up to 10% of the organization. They are found at all levels ... from the janitor to the C-suite. Look around you: 10% of your associates are naysayers.

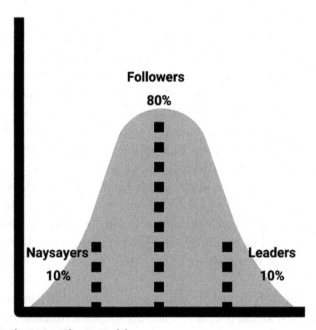

FIGURE 7.1 The Toyota Change Model

Art Byrne relayed his experience of an office product company from his time working in private equity. This $1 billion+ company that made all types of filing products (hanging and manila file folders, etc.) was brought to Art's attention by a bright, market-focused, strategic thinker who had now become the CEO after previously working for the company earlier in his career. Art couldn't get him to do Lean even though it was imperative to survive in an industry where sales were declining at about 4% per year, as laptops, iPads, and mobile phones were doing more of the "filing." A few years later, Art's private equity company sold the most profitable part of this company, a labeling business, which resulted in paying down all the debt and getting a 1.1 return on the investment. But, they now had a $1.1 billion company still in a declining market and only earning $15 million in EBITDA. Because Art's firm couldn't wait for the CEO to get with the program (he was essentially a naysayer), he was removed and replaced with a Lean-friendly, ex-Wiremold executive. From 2005 to 2013, using Lean, the new CEO steered EBITDA from $15 million to $85 million (even as sales fell to $850 million), freed up over $200 million in working capital and 2.2 million square feet of factory space, and grew the European business sales by 1%. Plus, the private equity firm realized a 3.5x return despite the poor market dynamics.

In Art's example, the naysayer was right at the top, which made the acquisition broken to begin with. It's a tough call to change out senior leadership but, after multiple attempts to get him on board, he wasn't interested in driving the necessary Lean changes that ultimately did prove to turn around performance when in the hands of an executive who championed them.

Naysayers must be given a chance to change. I love the expression, *"Change the People, or Change the People."* I have seen naysayers become the biggest promoters of Lean. However, I have also seen those who are unwilling to change. The fact is, there will be casualties during a Lean transformation and, after given a chance, naysayers must be asked to leave the organization if they refuse to change. Many times, naysayers are often the most technically competent, so leaders end up allowing them to exist unchecked within the organization. I once fired a very talented engineer and my colleagues could hardly believe it, but I knew his attitude was a kind of organizational cancer.

Leaders need to bear in mind that naysayers always do more harm than good, and they will derail your Lean transformation. A leader who allows a naysayer to survive is actually showing disrespect for the others within the organization. Ultimately, naysayers are underperformers. Leaders become underperformers as well if they allow naysayers to remain.

Companies that embark on a Lean transformation face the reality that their employees are not accustomed to permanently solving problems. They are typically engaged in putting out fires on a temporary basis and get their job satisfaction and recognition from putting out these fires. The new reward system must recognize the permanent prevention of problems (fires), instead of the mere elimination of them. When employees are not able to make this transition, they can become naysayers and casualties.

DEVELOP A HEALTHY DISSATISFACTION WITH THE STATUS QUO

Sometimes the culture is so established, it's difficult to change. "That's the way it has always been done" is often the mantra. Lean methodology, by nature, asks us to challenge the status quo. Recall the phrase that we coined at Danaher to represent the spirit of kaizen: "Anything that I'm doing today can be done better tomorrow." Without this fundamental belief radiating throughout the organization, improvements can't happen. The flatline will stay flat.

CASE STUDY

I went to see a company that was new to Lean. They made blow-molded plastic truck boxes and, while touring the plant, I noticed an inventory of boxes piled high all around. I asked the President and Vice President of Manufacturing why they had so much finished inventory on the shop floor. The VP stated that after the truck boxes come off the molding machine, they must cool and cure for 48 hours before being handled by downstream processes.

I asked if there was an engineering study to validate that the boxes needed to cure for 48 hours. The answer was no; however, the VP said that they know through experience that this is the right amount of curing time. So, I asked if the time could be shortened to 47 hours. They said that this should not be a problem. So, I went on to ask if 46 hours is acceptable. They said that this should be okay. I continued to ask: "What about 45? 44? 43?" I told them that I would continue to ask until they told me that the time was no longer acceptable. We discovered that the 48-hour policy was established ten years prior due to a quality problem with the customer. During that time, nobody challenged the policy. I asked them to do an engineering study and said I'd return at the end of the week to review their findings. During their presentation, they confirmed that I was right and that the curing time only needed to be 20 MINUTES! As a matter of fact, the process of stacking heavy, hot boxes on each other were causing defects to the products below.

We shut down production until the inventory was used up. This is a clear example that the status quo (in this case, the 48-hour cure time policy) was accepted and unchallenged for more than a decade.

Art Byrne shared another example of the need to overcome what he calls "the lore that exists in all companies." Years ago, he was on the board of a small jewelry manufacturer based in Florida. They made mostly rings for the middle market, with customers like JCPenney, Montgomery Ward, and Sears. The rings were made of gold and precious stones but sold in the $300–$600 price category. They were struggling and asked Art to come down to help. Art asked, "How long does it take to make a ring?" The answer was eight weeks. After Art asked why it could possibly take eight weeks, they replied that it was the standard in their industry. After speaking to other jewelry manufacturers, Art confirmed that it was indeed eight weeks for them as well.

Art asked the original company to show him the manufacturing process and they took a walk. He witnessed a mess in a dark and dusty, cave-like setting, where every single step in the process was done in a batch. Rings were delivered to individual operators, who were seated at a set station that did only one thing. After the operator finished that operation, the rings were taken back to the office, where they were counted and then stored before moving in a batch to the next process step. This was due to the value of the work in process to make sure that no gold or stones were disappearing. The washing and cleaning operation was a bottleneck because it had to happen several times in a separate room. They used the lost wax process and would wax up a batch of 100 of the same

rings at a time, embed them in a plaster of Paris mold, dry them overnight, melt the wax out the next day, and pour in the gold. After the
batch of 100 rings was finished, it went into their warehouse (a big safe)
and came out weeks later to a separate shipping department when they
had orders.

Art created the first cell-to-service for their largest customer, which
was JCPenney. They still waxed up 100 rings at a time but now they were
all different depending on the orders that came in that day. They still
dried them overnight and finished them the next day. Art put the shipping department right at the end of the cell, as it only took up a few feet
of bench space. The cell had 13 operators and his original calculations
(based on observations) were that it should be able to do 250 rings per
day. They added bright lighting and a new clean work environment that
made the cell stand out in the plant and made the operators proud to
work there. A large hour-by-hour production control board was installed
so everyone could see where they stood versus the target. At first, they
couldn't get to the 250 target, so they made changes and solved problems.
Then, one day at the end of the shift, a big cheer went up in the factory
when they had made the 250 goal. A few weeks later, there was another
cheer when the cell did 300. This continued until the same original team
of 13 was doing 450 rings every day.

Although this was a commendable productivity gain, the real story was
that the accepted "lore" of the prior eight-week lead time turned into two
days, which gave them a tremendous competitive advantage. This never
would have happened if they didn't ask for help from someone outside
their industry. Imagine if they went looking for a new VP of operations
instead, where, of course, part of the recruiting spec would be, "Must
have jewelry industry experience." That new VP would arrive with the
ingrained belief that it takes eight weeks to make a ring.

I have used this "Monkey Fable" to show how the "we have always
done it this way" culture gets created. A version of this tale seems to have
first been published in a book called *Competing for the Future* by Gary
Hamel and C.K. Prahalad (Harvard Business Review Press, reprint
edition, 1996). There wasn't a source, and it's doubtful this experiment
really took place. Even so, it provides an invaluable lesson to us all:

> Start with a cage containing five monkeys. Inside the cage, hang a banana
> on a string and place a set of stairs under it. Before long, a monkey will go
> to the stairs and start to climb toward the banana. As soon as he touches

the stairs, spray all of the other monkeys with cold water. After a while, another monkey attempts it with the same result: the other monkeys are sprayed with cold water. Pretty soon, when another monkey tries to climb the stairs, the other monkeys will try to prevent it.

Now, put away the cold water. Remove one monkey from the cage and replace it with a new one. The new monkey sees the banana and wants to climb the stairs. To his surprise and horror, all of the other monkeys attack him. After another attempt and attack, he knows that if he tries to climb the stairs, he will be assaulted.

Next, remove another of the original five monkeys and replace it with a new one. The newcomer goes to the stairs and is attacked. The previous newcomer takes part in the punishment with enthusiasm! Likewise, replace a third original monkey with a new one, then a fourth, then the fifth.

Every time the newest monkey takes to the stairs, he is attacked. Most of the monkeys that are beating him have no idea why they were not permitted to climb the stairs or why they are participating in the beating of the newest monkey.

After replacing all the original monkeys, none of the remaining monkeys have ever been sprayed with cold water. Nevertheless, no monkey ever again approaches the stairs to try for the banana.

Why not?

Because, as far as they know, that's the way it's always been done around here.

And that, my friends, is how company policy begins.

DELEGATE PROBLEM-SOLVING

I've come across many leadership teams who feel it's their responsibility to solve everyone's problems in the organization. Problems should be solved at the lowest possible, highest necessary level in the organization. The closest to the work/problem, the more likely the problem will be fully understood and a permanent solution will be implemented.

I learned the value of engaging the operator while walking through a manufacturing facility with my sensei, Mr. Chihiro Nakao of Shingijutsu. He stopped and noticed an operator processing parts on a machine with a cart containing his finished parts positioned about 15 feet away from the machine. This resulted in considerable walking for the operator. He looked puzzled when Nakao walked into the work area and moved the cart an additional 15 feet away from the operator. Nakao then left the area and we continued our tour. Approximately 45 minutes later, Nakao asked to go back to visit the operator. When we arrived at the work area, we saw the operator had moved the cart and positioned it right next to the machine.

Traditional management would have moved the cart themselves with the potential of the operator feeling demeaned. Nakao knew the right answer but wanted the operator to come up with the idea himself. Nakao believes that the operators are the best consultants who know the nature of the work better than anyone. This particular operator was never challenged to think and, through Nakao's unique way, was empowered to rethink his approach to work in a way that eliminated waste from walking.

To delegate problem-solving, those leaders with the big titles and big offices need to abandon the "smartest person in the room" complex. It's not about being the smartest or having the A-players. Toyota claims that it gets brilliant results from average people managing brilliant processes. In the universe of associates that are available, everyone can't be an A-player and that can be a good thing. Often, A-players are focused more on personal efforts than on building business processes that help the B-players shine, which in turn helps the team and organization. If only the highly skilled people are executing on quality, customer satisfaction, and profitability, the business will fail. Everyone has to be set up to execute well.

CASE STUDY

I encountered an organization that had a severe past-due backlog to the customer. When I suggested they put on a third shift as a way to eliminate the backlog, a vice president told me that it's not possible since it takes six months to train a factory operator. Upon further investigation, I found that this company's processes weren't documented, and no standard work existed. This company's culture was to rely on the tribal knowledge of their employees. This was fine until there was an early retirement program and all of the knowledgeable employees left the organization. Their lack of focus on process resulted in an untenable delivery situation with their customer base. Not only did leadership allow for their processes to be undocumented; they tolerated the fact that the processes were difficult for the operator to be successful.

For employees to be successful problem-solvers, leadership must provide the tools and training to those who are expected to solve the company's problems. An executive from Toyota once told me: "All companies have problems. Even world-class companies. What makes a world-class company is how effectively they solve problems. That's the ultimate difference."

SUMMARY

Become active in your Lean transformation and accept responsibility for it. Be willing to coach and teach others, as well as continually learn through hands-on participation in the Lean philosophies and tools. If your transformation is continuing to flatline, look in the mirror and consider that you may be the cause of the problem.

QUESTIONS TO ASK

- Do you and your leaders regularly participate in kaizen events within your organization?
- Do your leaders possess the necessary knowledge to ask the right questions?
- How do you demonstrate "respect for people" within your leadership style?
- Do you have defined requirements for leadership?
- Are you creating processes that put your values and principles into action?
- Have you developed non-negotiables for your organization?
- Are you allowing naysayers to remain in your organization?
- Does your organization have established protocols that no one ever questions?
- Does your organization have a standardized process for solving problems?
- Do you solve problems at the "lowest possible, highest necessary" level in your organization?
- Are those who are expected to solve the company's problems well equipped to do so?

8

Conclusion

The concepts shared in *Flatlined* can make businesses more efficient, productive, and customer-focused. The market gains better quality and service because businesses that can make and sustain turnarounds are more stable, competitive, and innovative. They also help the economy by creating job security and becoming less likely to look for cheap labor abroad. A healthy company is poised to be a good environmental steward and to care about their role in the community by supporting charities, veteran endeavors, and diversity programs.

Employ and keep revisiting the five steps covered in this book, and you will find that not only is your company not flatlining anymore, but that you are soon on an accelerated path to world-class status.

As you begin to take action on these steps, I've provided a checklist for what you need to have in place in the Addendum. I also want you to keep these three points at the forefront:

1. no silver bullets;
2. be Lean; don't do Lean;
3. call to leadership.

NO SILVER BULLETS

While it can be tempting at times to look for the quick answer, there are no silver bullets when it comes to Lean. For example, you may want to chase low labor rates, but that typically proves to be more costly in the long run. Instead of moving operations thousands of miles away and extending your lead times, you can lower overall labor costs by making your business more efficient, providing job security for your employees, and assuring that you are competitive in service, lead times, and quality for your customer base.

Some companies learn this the hard way. We conducted a supply chain study for a multibillion-dollar manufacturer of consumer goods who wanted to understand the viability of moving their manufacturing to Asia. At the conclusion of our assessment, we recommended that they not relocate their operations based on the "total cost of ownership" (TCO) and the potential disruption to customer service. Leadership was hoping that our recommendations matched their desire to relocate the operations. Their thought was to use an outside consulting firm, such as Lean Horizons, to sell their idea to senior leadership. We didn't agree with their proposition; however, their minds were made up even before they called us in, so they proceeded to move their operations regardless. Unable to deliver on time to their customer, Home Depot, they were billed $8 million in late-charge penalties. As a result of this mishap, seven of their executives were fired.

Automation of factories is another silver bullet that I have seen fail over the years. Many companies have moved to automation and robotics only to find that their operating costs have significantly increased and they've created severe quality, service, and delivery problems to their customers. I am not against automation provided it is used correctly and applied to a situation which warrants the use of automation. The pros and cons of automation are beyond the scope of this book, but suffice it to say that the decision to automate is typically misguided and, in the final analysis, a failure.

Another example of a silver bullet is the implementation of an ERP (enterprise resource planning) system. In general, there is nothing wrong with an ERP system provided that some of its components, such as MRP (manufacturing resource planning) do not violate fundamental Lean principles. These would include having single point scheduling, utilizing takt time, supporting a value stream approach to organizing a business, and allowing for Lean accounting practices. I have seen senior executives become convinced by software vendors that an ERP system will be the answer to all of their problems and that the financial returns are enormous. In all of my decades of interacting with thousands of companies, this has never been the case.

One of the most significant issues with the implementation of ERP is that businesses attempt to automate business processes that are wrought with waste. I once convinced a CEO of a $2 billion diversified manufac-turer to delay his ERP implementation by 18 months. My reasoning was that there was so much waste and non-standardization in his processes that the ERP implementation would be a total failure and he would spend at least 50% more on ERP than originally planned. (Note: His original budget to implement this ERP system was $80 million!) Although his ERP implementation team was extremely upset over the schedule delay, he finally agreed with me. We put together an aggressive plan to kaizen his various processes and took out a significant amount of waste. As an example, this company had 26 distribution facilities throughout North America. There were no standard processes to run these facilities, and it was highly questionable whether all were needed or were geographically positioned strategically to service their customer base. When we com-pleted our work, we were able to eliminate 60% of the distribution facili-ties. This saved them millions in ERP implementation fees and provided much lower operating costs and better service to their customer base overall. I will never contend that you should sway away from ERP, but its implementation should be thought through carefully, assuring that you have a sound business case.

I have seen many silver bullets come and go. Most, if not all, fail. It is important to conclude that Lean itself is not a silver bullet! Even if Lean is executed flawlessly, if your business model or strategy is flawed, you will not achieve the success desired. No matter what course we choose, it will require hard work, dedication, discipline and a commitment to continu-ally learn and evolve. One-time silver bullets do not fit these requirements.

BE LEAN; DON'T DO LEAN

I was asked to conduct a progress review for a plant in a company that had been "doing" Lean for over a decade—a plant considered to be the best Lean facility within this $13 billion global organization. As I spent the first day listening to the story of their journey and touring their facil-ity, it was clear they had all of the outward markings of a truly Lean organization, and senior management at the corporate office was con-vinced they'd done an outstanding job transforming their plant with Lean. It was also clear to me that they were not "being Lean."

Their management presented a myriad of metrics to show their "progress" compared with the prior year. In reality, this put a spotlight on many dysfunctional Lean behaviors, which you'll now recognize from the previous chapters in this book:

- They touted that their inventory turns increased from 6.5x to 18x. Upon further review, this increase in inventory "performance" was due to the fact that they placed 70% of their raw material inventory on consignment and did not count this inventory in their calculation. Regardless of whose books the inventory is valued on, the same ills of excess inventory exist. That this inventory was consigned encouraged the company to hold more inventory than they otherwise would have had it been purchased and valued on their own balance sheet. To make matters worse, the company extended their raw materials warehouse in order to accommodate the increase in raw material inventory.
- Management then said that their sales per employee productivity metric increased from $280,000 to $360,000. They explained that there was a renewed focus on standardized work, which accounted for most of this improvement. As I probed further, I learned that the company laid off 30% of its workforce the prior year and that overtime hours in the plant increased from 5% to 35% during this time period. Had they calculated their productivity based on hours worked, their improvement would have been negligible.
- Management revealed that their on-time delivery performance was 98%. We found this delivery performance was calculated based on their promise date to the customer within the company's stated six-week lead time. I counseled them on the fact that their promise date is meaningless to the customer and that they should switch their calculation to customer request date. They indicated that they have attempted to calculate it this way and that the actual on-time delivery performance using this method was only 35% to promise date. (They did not want to present this figure to their senior management, so the promise date figure was used.)

As we toured the facility, I saw it was spotless, well lit, and that one could have eaten off the painted floors. Many assembly cells were in place, which seemed orderly. I participated on their morning gemba walk to review the facility and the previous day's performance. I noticed the following:

- We first stopped at their gemba board, which contained all of their operating metrics and value stream information. Many of the metrics were posted without goals or targets, so it was difficult to gauge their performance. The value stream map information consisted of only the current state map, with no lead time ladder or future state map. There was no value stream plan, so kaizen events were not tied into achieving the future state condition.
- Although they constructed reasonably good manufacturing cells, the operators batched production and did not produce in a one-piece flow fashion. Operators were seated, which did not allow them to perform the required number of operations to consume their takt time.
- Standard work combination sheets were posted in each cell. The standard work was outdated, dated approximately one year prior. The original date was crossed out and just replaced with the current date. They had not updated it to reflect changes in takt time or kaizen improvements.
- Each cell tracked their production using hour-by-the-hour boards. Their previous day's planned production units were 100; however, they recorded an actual production quantity of 145 units. They marked this figure in green to reflect a favorable condition. When I asked why this figure was marked in green, they indicated that they exceeded their production plan and stated, "We had a good day." Now, every Lean practitioner is familiar with the seven wastes, one of which is waste from overproduction. I counseled them that this excess production should have been marked in red, as an abnormal condition. I further explained that if they were in fact properly using standard work, excess production would be virtually impossible (if operators are working to a properly calculated takt time).

This particular company was the most profitable within this $13 billion industrial. I believe that their superior profitability jaded leaderships' assessment of their Lean status. Many companies that have jumped on the continuous improvement bandwagon are similar to this example. While they do believe they are "doing" the right Lean things, and it will look like that to the uneducated eye, they have not internalized the mindset of "being" Lean.

The toughest businesses to change are those that are financially successful. While at Danaher, we had a division that was one of our most profitable, achieving 40% operating profit year after year. However, when we evaluated them on their Lean/DBS status, they were one of the worst in Danaher. Leadership of this division had delusions of grandeur regarding their overall competence, but they really happened to be in a market which provided fantastic margins. How much better could they have been if they fully adopted DBS? Well, we pointed out the waste they hadn't yet conquered and didn't give them a pass on DBS.

Gaining this experience to differentiate those who are "being Lean" from those who are "doing Lean" takes practice. Consider this story: While visiting a Toyota supplier in Japan, I asked the president how long it takes to change over his injection molding equipment. He replied, "It takes one minute. Would you like to see an actual changeover?" I told him that I did not want to impose since this would be a disruption to his production operation. He insisted and ordered his shop personnel to perform a changeover. I timed it, and it only took 55 seconds! The changeover crew then switched back to the original setup. As we walked away, the president said, "DeLuzio-san, thank you for giving us the opportunity to practice our changeover."

This story illustrates the difference between a traditional mindset versus a Lean mindset. Traditional companies typically try to avoid changeovers, resulting in large batch production runs, excess inventory, and poor on-time delivery. There is a direct correlation between lead time and changeover time. A changeover that is reduced by 50% will in fact reduce the lead time by 50%. Lean leaders should embrace the opportunity to do more changeovers because, if you think about how a NASCAR pit crew works from the "relate it back to real life" section, it's proven that changeover times decrease the more they are practiced. And this type of thinking can be applied to anything in Lean.

At Danaher, I discouraged our companies to pursue industry awards for Lean, with the only exception being customer-driven awards. There are several problems with such awards. First, preparing to win these awards takes your focus away from your business and your customer. These awards typically consist of "check the box" ratings that force the focus on areas that are not meaningful to the organization. Second, companies who win such awards adopt a mentality that they have "arrived," which is counter to the continuous improvement mindset that is essential to a Lean transformation. And finally, they cost money—money that can be better put to use elsewhere in the Lean journey. I am very proud to have been inducted into the Shingo Academy, the "Hall of Fame" of

Lean. However, I do not let this stymie my growth. After 30 years of practicing Lean, I still consider myself a student. I have not "arrived," nor will I ever. I still have a lot to learn!

Key to being Lean is also ensuring that you are focused on the right problem. I recall a time when I was brought in to address the waste in a call center that fielded calls from customers who had technical problems with their product. Customers were dissatisfied with experiencing excessive hold times, and the leader of this operation already had the solution in his mind. He wanted to put in a new phone system to alleviate the call wait time. I had a different idea. The leader of this operation never considered that when a customer needs to call his service center, it should be considered a defect.

I convinced him that instead of working to make the handling of defects more efficient, why don't we work to eliminate the need for a customer to call altogether? He agreed, and we started to track the reasons as to why a customer needed to call. We then held kaizen events to address the top defects. For example, there were many calls which involved the installation of their product because the instructions weren't clear. This problem virtually went away once we revised the instructions. Through focusing on the reasons for a customer call, we were able to eliminate calls to the service center by 45%. Has your management adopted the mindset that a call from a customer is abnormal as this company learned to do?

PUTTING THE CALL CENTER INTO PERSPECTIVE

Four consultants walk into a technical support call center. The manager is looking for a solution to efficiently process the high volume of customer calls.

- The technology consultant says: "You need to upgrade your phone system!"
- The Six Sigma consultant says: "Give me every piece of data on every phone call ever made to this call center!"
- The theory of constraints (ToC) consultant says: "We need to find the system constraint!"
- The Lean consultant says: "Why are your customers calling so much?"

When senior leaders become educated through hands-on involvement, they learn to ask the right questions and understand what "good looks like" by benchmarking outside their organization. Keep asking yourself: Is my organization "doing" Lean or are we "being" Lean?

CALL TO LEADERSHIP

I implore leaders to regularly look in the mirror and ask themselves:

- Is what we are doing at the company mindful of the Lean Trilogy?
- Are we cultivating the long-term health of the business?
- Do I know the basics tenets of Lean in a way that I can demonstrate?
- Would I be making these same types of decisions in my personal life?
- Am I asking the right questions?

We discussed the importance of making decisions through the lens of what's good for employees, customers, and shareholders (the Lean Trilogy) in Chapter 3. If these constituency groups are not benefiting, your Lean transformation will in fact fail. To reiterate, it has been my experience that most leaders primarily focus on shareholder return a majority of the time, have a half-hearted focus on the customer, and pay lip service to employees. This may sound harsh, as there are usually a flurry of leadership activities surrounding these groups. But when you critically analyze these endeavors, many are motivated by political correctness, especially when it comes to employees.

For example, in previous chapters, we touched on the merits of calculating on-time delivery performance based on customer "request" date as opposed to customer "promise" date. Few leaders I've met are open to using request date, which is a much more difficult metric to achieve. I have heard all of the reasons why request date is not applicable to their business. However, request date is the most customer-centric metric you can have as it relates to on-time delivery performance. Let's face it: A promise date is not the customer's date … it's the company's date. The reluctance to use request date is hard evidence that leadership is not committed to the success of their customers. Rather, they would rather use metrics that are meaningless in the eyes of their customer to make themselves look good as leaders.

Healthy, successful businesses are:

- people-driven: growing the business means your employees are secure and growing too—remember, people appreciate, machines depreciate;
- customer-focused;
- innovating: breakthrough breeds breakthrough;
- growing: this is only happening because fundamental operations are always improving to support that growth. It's like planning the garden, fertilizing the soil, and planting good seeds;
- good environmental stewards: they have the resources to promote corporate social responsibility and have a positive impact in the community;
- and finally, financially successful: note—I firmly believe that if you are not financially successful (and superior to your benchmarks), you cannot consider yourself a great company. I have noticed over the years that financial results do not get discussed enough when it comes to Lean transformations. As a matter of fact, I believe many Lean practitioners and business leaders are embarrassed to make money! I had a client who was only budgeting 2% operating profit for the year, and their plan was to achieve 10% in three years. The CEO was reluctant to incorporate profitability into his strategic breakthrough objectives. He stated that his employees did not care about the company's profitability and was concerned that the morale of his employees might be harmed if they knew that leadership was concerned with profitability. Ignoring for a moment that his specific profitability goals were lethargic at best, I challenged him on the notion that his employees need to understand why a profitable company was beneficial for employees and shareholders alike. This is a communication issue and it was no surprise to me that the profitability of this firm was abysmal after experiencing the low expectations the CEO and his leadership team had.

Know the basic tenets of Lean in ways that you can demonstrate. As I was preparing the agenda for a Lean bootcamp for a mid-sized manufacturer, the CEO asked why we needed to focus on the introduction to Lean principles and concepts. He felt that this would be redundant to his team and that they already understood the basics. (Note: After visiting a few of his factories, it was obvious they did not understand the basics.) I explained to the CEO that they may intellectually understand the concepts, but they don't know how to implement. I reminded him of Vince Lombardi when he began coaching the Green Bay Packers. Lombardi started his first practice with the statement: "Gentlemen, this is a football." Lombardi was a stickler for the basics and felt that if his team could not consistently implement the basics of football, they would never win a championship. Lombardi eventually took his team to a Super Bowl championship and became one of the greatest coaches in the history of the NFL

And, remember, the basics aren't just about the tools. It also has to do with acting in accordance with the Lean principles and ways of thinking. If this doesn't start with the CEO, your company will face challenges in using Lean for sustainable growth across the enterprise. You will not be able to convince the sales VP that the company should produce to customer demand versus a forecast. You will not be able to convince the CFO that we shouldn't build unnecessary inventory for the sake of favorable absorption variances. You will not be able to convince the production planning group that the company needs to abandon MRP batch-and-queue scheduling and move toward single-point scheduling. You will not convince the manufacturing VP that it is not in keeping with Lean principles to run production to optimize machine uptime and overall equipment effectiveness (OEE) as opposed to producing to takt time. I could go on and on. The point is, the company will continue to flatline on Lean if your leadership team does not evolve their traditional way of running a business into a way that is genuinely and comprehensively aligned with Lean principles.

I hope this book has provided you with some insight as to what it really takes to successfully reignite your Lean transformation. Is it easy? NO! If you have any doubt if it will be worth it, please take a look at benchmark companies like Toyota, Danaher, Fortive, and Wiremold. What's common across these companies is that their leadership is committed, actively involved, and extremely open to learning and change. Are you willing to be a leader who is committed, involved, and open to learning and change? If so, you have just made the vital decision which will lead you toward a successful Lean transformation. Congratulations, and I look forward to hearing about your journey!

Addendum

What You Must Have in Place
for Your Lean Transformation

- The mindset of fully adopting Lean (not chasing other solutions/ quick wins)
- A plan to uphold the Lean Trilogy
- A willingness for leaders to learn and become actively involved
- A CEO who accepts full responsibility for their Lean transformation
- A head of Lean who reports to the CEO
- Organization by value streams
- An effective, qualified Lean organization at the corporate office, as well as throughout the various businesses/divisions/locations in the company
- A Lean organization that builds internal capability by the practice of "teaching others to fish"
- An environment where the focus is on problems with the process rather than assigning blame to employees
- A focus on "process-based" results rather than results alone
- A robust strategic planning process, identifying breakthrough objectives that are implemented through the strategy deployment process
- Continual benchmarking to world class (looking outside your industry)
- The experience to know you are solving the right problems
- A drive from point kaizen improvements to enterprise kaizen transformations
- Willingness to challenge traditional management practices, policies and organization structure, looking to eliminate mura and muri within the organization
- Abandonment of traditional accounting practices, such as standard costing, and adopting Lean accounting principles and practices
- Insisting that problems within your organization are solved at the "lowest level possible and highest level necessary"

- Establishment of "non-negotiable" guidelines for all to follow
- The willingness to divorce the organization from naysayers, regardless of their talent level

Lean Horizon's Lean Leadership Bootcamp Agenda

Topic	Lecture	Discussion / Exercise
Welcome/Introduction/Agenda Review		
Role of Executive Leadership – Creating a Culture of Change and Change Management	●	●
Lean Principles	●	
Lean Accounting and Accounting for Lean – Case Study	●	●
A Deeper Dive into S&OP	●	●
A Word on Strategy Deployment and Metrics	●	●
What to Expect from a Lean Enterprise	●	
Lean Benchmarks – Financial and Operational	●	
Decoding the DNA of the Toyota Production System – Where Do You Stack Up?	●	●
Setting Expectations		●
People – Evaluating Your "Bus"		●
Elements of a Lean Transformation		
Doing Lean versus. Being Lean		●
Wrap-up and Next Steps		●

WHAT YOU SHOULD LOOK FOR IN A LEAN COACH OR CONSULTANT

Today's Lean industry consists of thousands, if not millions, of Lean consultants whose competency varies widely. Let's review the factors you should consider and questions to ask when selecting a Lean consultant or coach:

- Does the consultant have "brownfield" experience? In other words, have they implemented Lean transformations within well-established, traditionally run companies that are brand new to adopting Lean principles? We have found that consultants who only have "greenfield" experience (executing Lean in a company that has a rather well-established Lean program, such as Toyota) struggle when faced with implementing Lean in a brownfield environment.

- Does the consultant have ties back to the original founding of the Toyota Production System? It is important to understand their lineage and where they learned and gained their Lean experience.
- Does the consultant have *successful* Lean transformation experience? Many consultants enter the Lean consulting industry with experience limited to running kaizen events. It amazes me that CEOs look to these people to help them lead a full Lean transformation. I would say most Lean consultants do not have transformation experience, let alone *successful* transformation experience.
- Does the consultant commit to "teach you and your people how to fish?" In other words, do they have a process to transfer knowledge to your organization? Developing a Lean organization within the company requires great teaching and facilitation skills.
- Does the consultant have tacit, hands-on experience? You need to ensure that they don't mainly possess explicit (book) knowledge and that they have actual implementation experience with a Lean transformation. Ask for examples and case studies, including the specific role the consultant played and at what level (i.e., the shop floor, administration). Remember, success has many fathers and failure is an orphan.
- Does the consultant have the ability to coach senior leadership to understand how to deploy a strategy and align Lean efforts to support the strategy?
- Does the consultant possess business experience or are they solely Lean zealots? You need both.
- Does the consultant have experience with designing a Lean organization for your company?
- Does the consultant promote Lean basics or are they attempting to sell you some silver bullet that will take you and your organization away for the basics?
- Finally, if you, as a CEO or senior executive, are looking to hire a Lean coach, does the consultant have experience in dealing with senior leadership?

Index

Page numbers in *italic* denote figures and in **bold** denote tables.

Printed in the United States
by Baker & Taylor Publisher Services